TESTIMONIALS

The amount of Ah-ha moments I had while reading Bill Blokker's *Achieve Beyond Expectations* is enough to make me want to read it over and over. As a leader in my industry that has always been intrinsically motivated, I've struggled with effectively supporting my team in a way that builds the confidence they need to succeed. This book is going to be my literal blueprint in helping us create positive habits, healthy self-talk and an unwavering belief in ourselves... You will finish this book ridiculously inspired, ready to implement and share Bill's easy to learn lessons and with serious excitement to see the changes in both you and in those you lead!
   — Melissa McAllister, NTP CEO Team M.A.D.E. International

In this exceptional read, Bill Blokker educates and motivates the reader through real life examples of how everyday people have overcome incredible odds to achieve their dreams. Blokker's many years studying human behavior and leadership make him qualified. Highly recommended for anyone who wants to improve their own lot in life or those who they influence. You won't be disappointed!
   — Craig Whelden Major General, U.S. Army (retired)

Several years ago, Bill took me under his wing and mentored me professionally. He personally taught me the practical and proven principles he had utilized in his own highly successful career to help me take my career to the next level, exceeding what I had dreamed possible. In this book, Bill expands upon those powerful principles in a very engaging, entertaining, and practical way. I highly recommend this book to anyone who is serious about taking full advantage of the one life you've been given to achieve the impossible and dramatically impact the world around you.
   — Doug Fitzgerald, Life Coach and CEO, ONESHOT.ONELIFE

As a business owner and corporate executive, today's challenging business climate requires every top executive to be fit both mentally and physically. To take yourself and your organization to the next level, you must always think beyond that next level. *Achieve Beyond Expectations* shows you how to do just that.
   — Ed Dare, President and CEO, Partners Financial Group

The perfect blend of science, insight, and inspiration that can be applied to any aspect of your life. If you want to see change, you have to put in the work and Bill makes this very tangible. He does a phenomenal job of providing a foundation not only for improving your life but how to apply your learnings to "make the impossible, possible." If you want to change any aspect of your life – personal or professional, this is the perfect book for you!

> — Michelle Tatom, Director Global Account Management,
> SkyKick

An in-depth how-to that digs into a number of common obstacles that keep us from attaining all our life goals. Blokker unpacks easy-to-miss behaviors and mindsets that stifle our potential in every facet of life. The main idea: stop making excuses so you can make changes, no matter what you might be facing. Blokker's approach to reacting productively to the most unexpected bumps in the road is a timely and much-needed message as we maneuver though historically troubling times. This book brings all its concepts to the ground by using real world examples and SHOWING how they work. This book is both a wake-up call and a long-term solution to finding real success!

> — Cassandra Woody, Assistant Teaching Professor,
> University of Oklahoma

Easy to read and thoroughly systematic for how to achieve excellence in your life. The challenging part is that it forces you to do the actual self-awareness growth work, so it's not for the faint of heart but for those who really want to move to the next level personally and professionally. As someone who works with start-ups and consults with executives, I can see using it as a developmental textbook of sorts, a resource that would help any budding leader grow into their fuller potential.

> — Milo de Prieto, Branding and Communication Consultant,
> Barcelona, Spain

Blokker helps you to understand that regardless of your background and the hardships you have faced, you can still go on to achieve greatness. All you have to do is apply yourself and master the 5 intangibles. I recommend this brilliantly written book for anyone who wants to shine.

> — Olivia Stasi, Personal Trainer/ Beachbody Coach,
> United Kingdom

ACHIEVE
BEYOND
EXPECTATIONS

ACHIEVE
BEYOND
EXPECTATIONS

Master the **5** Intangibles
to Make the Impossible, Possible!

Bill Blokker, EdD

New Insights Press

New Insights Press
Editorial Direction and Editing: Rick Benzel
Cover and Book Design: Susan Shankin
Published by New Insights Press, Los Angeles, CA

First edition printed in the United States of America
ISBN: 978-1-7338411-7-7 (print)
       978-1-7338411-8-4 (eBook)
Library of Congress Control Number: 2020910775

DEDICATION

This book is dedicated to all of you willing to live on the edge.
To do whatever it takes to make the impossible, possible!
You are the ones who make all our lives better.

TABLE OF CONTENTS

Introduction

Achieve Beyond Expectations is written to inspire and inform you. This book is for you if you identify with any of these groups:

- **Achiever:** no matter your present situation or occupation in life, you have a desire to excel. You love challenges—the bigger the better. You want to be the best you can be.

- **Dissatisfied**: you have not yet accomplished things you want to accomplish. You feel as if you always fall short of your dream. No matter what you do, you just don't feel fulfilled.

- **Trauma**: you or a family member experienced an unexpected traumatic event. This could include things like injury, illness, divorce, or financial problems. You need to find a way to work through the morass of problems you're facing.

- **Parent**: you have a desire to be the best parent you can be, but you realize it is a far more challenging job than you ever imagined. You want to feel better

prepared to deal with the present and future challenges that parenthood brings.

- **Leader**: you are the formal or informal head of a
group of children or adults who expect you to provide
direction and support to accomplish your common
goals. You want to improve your knowledge and
skills to lead them in a productive manner.

When I studied high-achieving people and organizations, I found many commonalities. The most important
finding was that execution transcends talent. Many talented people were dominated by people with less talent.
What separated the extraordinary from the ordinary was
that the extraordinary applied five intangibles that caused
their performance to soar.

Life is complex. Complex situations require complex
solutions. Most complex situations are caused by your lack
of awareness of these five intangibles and their concealed
workings in your brain and body. The five intangibles are:
self-awareness, emotional control, habits, expectations and
self-efficacy. If you are unaware of these or do not know
how to manage them effectively, they will create self-imposed barriers to any change you want to make.

It is very common that you create your own problems!
To resolve that, each chapter of this book provides you with
valuable insights into the brain and human performance.
More importantly, you will be challenged to assess your
thinking and behavior. You will become more aware of areas
you need to change or reinforce. The book provides you with
in-depth information about how to make the changes necessary to accomplish your goals.

Now let's get real. Making the impossible, possible, is
neither quick nor easy! If you want a quick or easy fix, you

will not find it in this book. The reason: there is no quick or easy fix for any major accomplishment in life. Whether you embark on a major change in your life, or you experience an unexpected trauma, it will take time and effort to succeed.

This book is written like an instruction manual or a cookbook. Each chapter provides a wealth of research-based information to create awareness of the concealed workings of your brain and body. Unbeknownst to you, these concealed workings determine your reality. To make significant changes in your life, you must become aware of and control the intangibles that control your every thought, emotion, and behavior.

Achieve Beyond Expectations is a no-nonsense book that straight out tells you there are no excuses. You can learn to control situations, or at the very least control your reactions to situations. The book continually reinforces that what matters in life is not what happens, but *your reaction* to what happens!

Try as you may, you cannot prevent negative things from happening to you. The key to achieving beyond expectations is to be aware of what is happening and then adjust your thinking and behavior to overcome whatever obstacle is in the way.

You can achieve beyond expectations. You can make the impossible, possible!

1

Execution Transcends Talent

Wilma Rudolph contracted polio at age five. She was physically disabled for much of her early life. Wilma wore a brace on her left leg until she was 12. Wilma Rudolph won multiple Olympic gold medals. In the 1960s, she was proclaimed the fastest female athlete in the world. Wilma Rudolph achieved beyond expectations.

A quarterback who played football at the University of Michigan was the 199th player picked in the National Football League draft in 2000. No one thought he was an outstanding talent. Tom Brady became the quarterback who lead the New England Patriots to nine Super Bowls, winning six of them. Many experts consider Brady the greatest quarterback of all time. Brady made the impossible, possible!

WHAT CAUSED these people to be so successful? *Execution transcends talent.* As you progress through this book you will be reading about many people who made the impossible, possible. They performed incredible feats. In all cases, their talent was not the foremost factor in their success. What separates the extraordinary from the ordinary is their ability to execute at the highest level during the most challenging times.

What does this mean? Here's an example. You just purchased an expensive, fancy blender—the kind that slices, dices, chops, mixes, blends, and pulverizes anything you put into it. It has all the "talent" you want and need. You get home and try to use it. You discover that it works only at the lowest level, with none of those whiz-bang, high-powered features! To say you are disappointed is an understatement. The blender has so much "talent," but it cannot execute!

You take it back to get a refund. You go to the returns counter and tell the clerk you're not happy and want your money back because the blender is not executing to its full potential. You can't use all of its "talents." It only operates at the lowest and slowest level.

The clerk apologizes and says she will gladly refund your money. "But," she adds, "we have seen this problem before. Let me see if I can get this thing to execute to its full potential." She takes a small panel off the back of the blender, sticks in a screwdriver and gives it a couple turns. She puts the panel back on and plugs in the blender. Voilà! The blender roars to life and executes to its full potential! You can now use all of its talents. The clerk explains how they had found that one of the wires comes loose during shipping. If they tighten the wire, the blender executes the way it was designed.

The same is true for humans. People can have all the talent in the world, but if they have any loose wires, they don't perform to their full potential. Think about your past experiences. Was there a time you wanted to do something really important, but it didn't work out as well as you wanted? It may have been taking a test or completing a project in school or creating a presentation for your job. How about a wedding proposal or asking the boss for a raise? When you did one of these and it failed to meet your expectations, were there a few "loose wires" that caused you to stumble or mumble?

~

"Fear and self-doubt have always been
the greatest enemies of human potential."
Brian Tracy

~

If there is a loose wire inside the brain, you can't execute and use all of your talents. There are many types of loose wires. One could be that you become overwhelmed with emotion. As a result, you perform poorly or not at all. Or the loose wire is a lack of self-efficacy, the belief in your own ability to be successful. In this case, you give just a half-hearted attempt. The loose wire could be that all your friends and family are insisting it's crazy to attempt a certain thing. You finally believe them and give up.

The people who achieve beyond expectations make sure all of their wires are tight. They do this by paying attention to the intangible knowledge and skills needed in their brain so they can perform at their highest level.

Two Categories of Achievement

Before we get further into the essence of this book, let us clarify what type of achievements we are discussing. There are two categories of people who achieve beyond expectations:

- The first is when someone does something as a spontaneous, one-time event that is normally unimaginable. This achievement is totally random and unplanned.
- The second is when someone intentionally and consciously works over an extended time to accomplish a significant goal.

Here are examples of spontaneous, one-time events.

In 2016, Eric Heffelmire was lying under his pickup truck in his garage, repairing a brake line on one of the wheels. The truck fell off the jack, pinning him under it. There was an explosion and the truck caught fire. His daughter, 19-year-old Charlotte Heffelmire was at home. She rushed to the garage and lifted the burning truck off her father. She then got into the burning truck and drove it on three wheels out of the garage.

There is no doubt this is achieving beyond expectations. How does a 19-year-old female lift a burning, 4,000-pound pickup truck so someone can get out from under it? She did it! Charlotte made the impossible, possible!

Aron Ralston was hiking by himself in Utah. He somehow dislodged a boulder that pinned his right arm against the canyon wall. For five days, he tried everything imaginable to free his arm, but with no success. There was only one solution. He used a dull pocketknife to amputate his arm at the elbow! Once he had broken the bones and cut through the skin and muscle, he then had to get out of the canyon. This included hiking seven miles and rappelling down a 65-foot cliff using only one hand!

To say Aron Ralston achieved beyond expectations is an understatement! His story became the basis for the 2010 movie *127 Hours*. There is no doubt, Aron Ralston made the impossible, possible.

~

"Impossible only means
that you haven't found the solution yet."
Anonymous

~

These one-time spontaneous events are unplanned, yet clearly awe-inspiring. They demonstrate unbelievable human capabilities and strength of character. They reflect immense courage, conviction, and capacity to do whatever it takes to achieve. Most of us have no idea of our capacity until our backs are against the wall.

This book focuses on the second category of achievement— when people intentionally and consciously work over an extended time to accomplish a significant goal or to overcome an unexpected challenge. These situations may take months or years to work through. Here are examples of long-term goals for which people might seek to achieve beyond expectations:

- lose 30 pounds and live a healthier lifestyle
- get out of an abusive relationship
- win the battle against breast cancer
- have a child using in vitro fertilization and a surrogate mother
- spend more time with your family
- permanently stop a substance abuse
- be the first person in your family to graduate from college
- care for an elderly parent
- deal with the unexpected death of a significant other
- shoot par golf despite a physical handicap
- rehabilitate a broken relationship with a significant other
- get training necessary for a better-paying job
- learn to knit so you can make a sweater for a dear friend's first baby
- save money to buy a new car or a home

There are thousands of other examples. The definition of achieving beyond expectations is different for every person. The common denominator: *people accomplish something that most think unlikely, improbable, or impossible given the circumstances.* All these goals will take time to accomplish. In addition, there will be many challenges to overcome as you work to accomplish the goal.

You define what it means to achieve beyond expectations. You are the person working to make the impossible, possible to better your life. You are the person deciding to accomplish something you have never done before. You are the one trying to work through a difficult life event. You are the one on the edge. Others may not view your situation as anything special. *It does not matter what they say or think!* You are choosing to achieve beyond your expectations, so you are the only one that matters.

What matters in life is not what happens,
BUT YOUR REACTION to what happens!

How Do You Achieve Beyond Expectations?

When doing the research for this book, I studied over 100 people who achieved beyond expectations. They came from every walk of life. They were all races and ethnicities. Some people lost over 150 pounds. Others overcame long-term substance abuse. There were inventors who made significant contributions to society. Others excelled against oppressive cultural norms. There were athletes, musicians, dancers, electricians, doctors, lawyers, farmers, military, and many others. All of their achievements took extended time and effort. They continuously faced significant obstacles that challenged them emotionally, intellectually, and physically.

These people demonstrated something that may surprise you: their achievement had only a little to do with raw talent, and nothing to do with the circumstances of their birth, race/ethnicity, gender, financial situation, handicapping conditions, physical size, or education.

You will find in their stories that achievement has to do with how they went about implementing the five intangibles that separate the extraordinary from the ordinary. These intangibles are the components of execution, and mastering them is why, in the end, *execution transcends talent*. The five intangibles are:

- Self-Awareness
- Emotional Control
- Habits
- Expectations
- Self-Efficacy

My research and personal experience show that people who achieve beyond expectations do so because they have mastery over these five intangibles that control execution. Human performance, in the best of conditions, is complicated. In high-pressure or stressful situations, it becomes much more complex. Behavior is triggered at a subconscious level. For the most part, your actions and words just happen! The five intangibles are driving those actions and words at the subconscious level.

Execution transcends talent. The effectiveness of your execution is dependent on you being "consciously competent" about all you do. When you are consciously competent, you are aware of what you are doing and why you are doing it. You are purposefully applying specific knowledge and skills to control your emotions, thinking, and behavior to get the desired results. It also means that you monitor your performance and adjust if necessary. People who are consciously competent can describe in detail what they did, why they did it, and the adjustments they can make when not getting the desired results.

The goal of this book is to inspire you and provide you with the knowledge/skills to execute at the highest level. To do that, you must be consciously competent about the five intangibles. In this book you will learn:

- the reasons why the five intangibles are so powerful and important;

- how they can manipulate you if you let them;

- how to control them so you can be in charge of your life.

~

"The only person you are destined to become
is the person you decide to be."
Ralph Waldo Emerson

~

To achieve beyond expectations requires far more than talent. Overcoming the obstacles requires control of the intangibles that impact the use of talent. Here is an example of how the intangibles were far more critical to success than the person's talent:

In 1932, he was only the fourth African American to receive an appointment to the U.S. Military Academy at West Point. Throughout his four years at the Academy, he was the only African American cadet. During that time, he experienced racial isolation from white classmates. They tried to drive him out of the Academy by using the "silent treatment." He never had a roommate. He ate meals by himself. He was considered the "invisible man."

Despite all this, in 1936, Benjamin O. Davis Jr. graduated from the United States Military Academy. He earned the respect of classmates. The West Point yearbook described him with these words: The courage, tenacity, and intelligence with which he conquered a problem incomparably more difficult than plebe year won for him the sincere admiration of his classmates.

Benjamin O. Davis Jr. went on to be in the first class of 13 African Americans to receive pilot training at Tuskegee Institute. Davis was one of only five who graduated from that initial class. He flew 60 combat missions in WWII for the Tuskegee Airmen and became their most famous commander. Davis was the first African American general officer in the U.S. Air Force. In 1998, he was promoted to a four-star general. There is no doubt that General Benjamin O. Davis Jr. achieved beyond expectations.

To succeed, it was critical for General Davis to have mastery of the intangibles. By controlling them, he was able to use his talent to its highest level. If he had failed to control his intangibles, his talent would have been inconsequential.

What to Expect of This Book

This book is for people who want to change a life situation. You may want to learn how to have more control in your life. Perhaps you want to excel in business, athletics, music, or other professional endeavor. You may be working to overcome a traumatic or unexpected challenging event. The book provides you with the "how-to" strategies to succeed.

It is often said that knowledge is power! However, as Eric Thomas rephrased it, "Knowledge is not power; *applied knowledge is power*." The woman who fixed the blender had the knowledge and she applied it to fix the loose wire. Without application of the knowledge, the blender would not work properly. With the how-to strategies in this book, you will gain the knowledge to fix any "loose wires." The question is, will you apply the strategies? If you do, you can achieve beyond expectations.

This book is designed as an instruction manual, a cookbook, or blueprint. It is not meant to be read in one quick gulp. You are urged to read just one chapter at a time. Each chapter has self-assessments to create awareness of your strengths and needs. There are detailed how-to strategies to grow and change your behaviors. Do the assessments and activities in that chapter. Apply the information from that chapter in your daily life for a while. Once you feel comfortable with that content, move on to the next chapter.

The chapters are organized to lead you from mastering one new set of strategies to another and then the next. By progressively implementing the content, you will lay a solid foundation to achieve beyond expectations. The content is designed to cause you to become consciously competent about the hidden workings of your brain and body that affect your performance. When you apply this knowledge and skill, you will realize that you can make the impossible, possible!

Making a life change means overcoming many obstacles. Recognize this journey is neither quick nor easy! If you want a rapid fix, you are not being realistic. There is no fast way to achieve any major accomplishment in life. This idea is reinforced when you read about the people highlighted in the book.

Think about any change you want to make as a major construction or remodel project. From the initial idea to the finished product, it can take 18 months to many years.

The larger and more complex the project, the more time and effort needed. You can make attempts to speed up the process, but some things just take time to get done. If you are trying to make a major change in your life or deal with a significant trauma, it is going to require time, positivity, patience, and persistence.

Components of Human Performance

How is it that you can work so hard at being successful and not be happy with the results? Your frustration might grow because others seem to be doing it so easily. It is irritating that a strategy you used successfully in the past is not working now.

Human performance is extremely complex. Research on human performance is ever growing and changing. The more we learn about how we function, the more complicated it gets. The simplest act requires a multitude of brain/body interactions, over 90% of which are at the subconscious level! In other words, we frequently are not aware of what causes us to do things the way we do them. We just do it!

~

"Knowing yourself is the beginning of all wisdom."
Aristotle

~

Let's take a big-picture view of the major mechanisms impacting human performance. With this information, you will have a deeper understanding of

- why we say execution transcends talent;
- how the five intangibles come into play to control your performance.

We begin with talent. All human performance requires us to develop technical knowledge and skills to achieve our goal. This is our talent. Electricians develop talent by first completing a training program, then an apprenticeship, and finally they become master electricians. No matter your profession—nursing, sales, music, law, farming, athletics, or business—you must develop your talent, the technical knowledge, and skills to do your job.

We must also develop talent for things we do other than our occupations. If you are a parent, you develop new knowledge and skills to parent effectively. What about if you want to permanently lose 30 pounds? Or perhaps you want to rehabilitate a difficult relationship. Perhaps you are suddenly thrust into performing as a primary caregiver for a family member with health issues. In each one of these situations, you must develop talent, knowledge, and skill to do the job. Talent is needed for all effective human performance.

In addition to talent, effective human performance is dependent on our ability to monitor and adjust our behavior as circumstances change. No matter your goal in life, you will face obstacles or need to solve problems. Seldom do you set out to accomplish a task and it all goes smoothly with no glitches. We all know that #*^! happens! To succeed with any task, you must monitor and adjust the use of your talent to get the results you want.

When we say monitor and adjust, it means you make an attempt at a task, then you

- observe the results;
- determine the next actions needed to accomplish the goal.

If you like what you see, you reinforce the good things and move on. If you are not getting the results you want, you assess *all* aspects of your behavior to determine how you are going to adjust or change your strategies.

Self-awareness greatly impacts human performance. It is the most important of the five intangibles. Your ability to monitor and adjust is dependent on your self-awareness. It allows you to become conscious about your thoughts, emotions, and actions.

Your effectiveness is dependent on how well you have developed your self-awareness skills. There is a surface-level awareness. This is when you are aware that you successfully assembled a desk you bought from IKEA. But what counts is really a deeper level of self-awareness about the task. The deeper level of self-awareness and the most important, is how the intangibles impacted your behavior as you assembled the desk. This means being aware of how your emotions, habits, expectations, and self-efficacy impact performance.

Let's say you really hate having to assemble things, but you can't afford to buy the expensive pre-assembled furniture. So your emotions are already playing a role in the assembly process. Your mindset about the desk assembly is, "I hate this. I always get confused and frustrated. I know I'm going to mess up!" Self-awareness about your emotions in this situation is critical. If you are aware that you have this negative emotional reaction, you can adjust your behavior to take control of your emotions. If you are unaware of your emotional reaction, it is not possible to adjust and take control.

*"You decide if emotions get in
your way or lead your way."*
Bill Blokker, EdD

How the Five Intangibles
Impact Human Performance

The five intangibles that drive human performance are: self-awareness, emotional control, habits, expectations and self-efficacy. They are diagrammed in a four-quadrant grid to help you understand how they interact with each other and impact your level of achievement. Take a look at the graphic labeled Human Performance to see how it works.

HUMAN PERFORMANCE

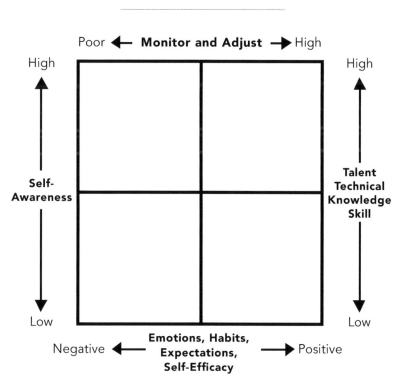

Talent, which is your technical knowledge and skill, appears on the right. Notice the arrows pointing up and down to high and low talent. Across the top of the grid is monitor and adjust. Here the arrows point to poor and high monitor/adjust skills. On the left side of the grid is the intangible, self-awareness, also with high and low arrows. On the bottom is a grouping of the four other intangibles—emotions, habits, expectations, and self-efficacy, with the arrows pointing to negative and positive. These four are on the bottom of the graphic to symbolize that they are foundational. One or more of these four impact every aspect of your behavior in a positive or negative way. These four intangibles can work independently or in collaboration with each other to impact behavior.

The four sides reflect the components of human performance. The factors all interact with each other to create four levels of performance that show how execution transcends talent. Note that descriptions are not a characterization of a person but rather of levels of performance.

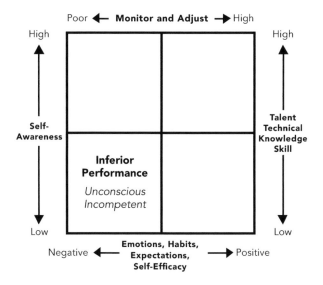

In the lower left is Inferior Performance, which results from:

- low talent
- low self-awareness
- poor ability to monitor and adjust
- negative emotions, habits, expectations, self-efficacy

The person performing a task in this category is an "Unconscious Incompetent." This person doesn't know he lacks knowledge to perform successfully. He has a negative mindset. He doesn't care about or sees no value in accomplishing the task.

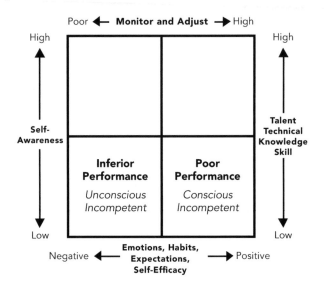

In the lower right is Poor Performance, which results from:

- low talent
- low self-awareness
- high ability to monitor and adjust
- positive emotions, habits, expectations, self-efficacy

The person performing a task in this category is a "Conscious Incompetent." She has an awareness that she doesn't have the talent needed to succeed. However, she is positive about her ability to develop whatever is needed to be successful.

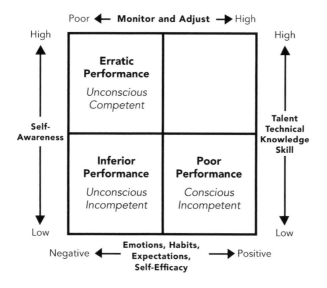

In the upper left is Erratic Performance, which results from:

- high talent

- high self-awareness

- poor ability to monitor and adjust

- negative emotions, habits, expectations, self-efficacy

The person performing a task in this category is an "Unconscious Competent." He performs well at times and poorly at other times. He does not know what he does to get good results or bad results. He experiences negative emotions because of the erratic performance.

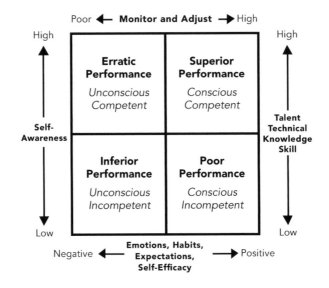

In the upper right is Superior Performance, which results from:

- high talent
- high self-awareness
- high ability to monitor and adjust
- positive emotions, habits, expectations, self-efficacy

The person performing a task in this category is a "Conscious Competent." She can repeat behaviors at will. No matter the obstacle presented, she has the knowledge and skills to adjust her behavior to succeed.

~

"Having a vision for what you want is not enough.
Vision without execution is hallucination."
Thomas A Edison.

~

Execution transcends talent. Your ability to use your talent depends on your awareness of the interactions of the mechanisms described in the Human Performance graphic. Your talent, ability to monitor/adjust, self-awareness, emotions, habits, expectations, and self-efficacy are continually interacting with each other to impact your performance.

The five intangibles are either working for you or ganging up on you. They are a well-honed team. It's up to you to learn to make them work in your favor. They can collaborate at lightning speed to grab onto all aspects of your behavior and take you in a direction you don't want to go!

For instance, what is your emotional and habitual response when something does not go as you expected on a task? Some people get frustrated and angry and say, "#*^! it," then quit. But people who can control the five intangibles stay calm, analyze what has happened, establish a new direction and proceed to accomplish the task. How about when you experience a unique or unexpected challenge? Some people look at it as an adventure, a way to demonstrate how capable they are. Others become overwhelmed and paralyzed with negative emotions.

As you read about the people highlighted in this book, it will be obvious that they had to take control of the five intangibles so they could succeed. Thousands more have learned how to take charge of these five intangibles. You can, too.

This book has a chapter dedicated to each of the five intangibles. The essence of each chapter details how they impact you and how you can learn to control them. You will learn what triggers your behaviors and how you can apply the information to real-life situations. The goal is for you to become consciously competent about these intangibles so you can take charge of your life.

~

"Second by second you lose the opportunity to become the person you want to be. Take charge of your life."
Greg Pitt

~

You Must Pay the Price

If you are reading this book, you may want to achieve beyond expectations or at least create a better life for yourself. Perhaps you want to start your own business. Maybe your goal is weight loss or developing a stronger relationship with a significant other. Whatever the change, large or small, there is always a price to pay.

Seldom do we get something of significant value and it costs nothing. Something of significant value can be a person, physical object, a relationship, an award, a pet, a lifestyle, or a state of mind. You always pay a price for something of significant value. The currency you use to pay the price will be different depending on the situation. The currency can be money, time, physical effort, emotional effort, or intellectual effort.

~

"You will find that everything in life exacts a price, and you will have to decide whether the price is worth the prize."
Sam Nunn

~

Check your awareness about the price you pay for a change you have made in your life. This activity will lead you through several self-awareness steps.

Using a Journal for the Activities

You will find many activities in this book that ask you to reflect on various aspects of your life and write down your thoughts and emotions. You may wish to use a separate journal for these activities in order to answer the questions more fully rather than writing brief answers in the book. A journal will also add to the privacy of your answers.

Activity: The Price You Pay for Change

Think about changes you have made successfully and ones where you have not succeeded. Important note: the effectiveness of this activity is dependent on *how honestly you respond to the questions*—no sugar coating, no embellishments. State what really happened rather than what you hoped would happen.

1. In your journal, draw a line down the middle of the page. At the top of the left column, write down a change you made *that was successful.* At the top of the right column, write down a change *that was not successful.*

2. Next, write down in each column *the reason* you wanted to make the change. How was your life situation to improve?

3. Next, write down in each column *how you increased your talent* (i.e., your knowledge/skills), so you could successfully make the change. Here are some categories to consider in your answers:

   a. Reading books or online materials

   b. Online training or classroom course

   c. Hired a coach or mentor to work with you

   d. Talked with people who succeeded in making the same change

4. Next, write down in each column *the price you paid* to make the change, whether it was successful or not. Here are some categories of currency you might have used to pay for the change:

   a. Money—how much?

   b. Time spent—hours, days, months or years you worked to make change

   c. Consistency of your effort—hourly, daily, weekly

   d. How much positive or negative emotional energy expended?

   e. How much intellectual energy impacted your effort?

   f. How much physical energy impacted your effort?

5. Summarize your total effort for each attempted change.

   a. What price did you pay for success? Was it worth it?

   b. What price did you pay for lack of success?

   c. How does the price you paid for success compare to the price you paid when unsuccessful?

What have you learned about yourself because of this activity? Write in your journal a few important things you want to reinforce because you did them well. Write down a few things you want to change so you will have more success in the future.

Here is one more thought to consider. When people are not successful, a major reason is they believe the price they are paying outweighs the value they think they will get. So, they stop paying!

When you quit, you have already paid a huge price and will get nothing for it. This leads to negative thoughts and emotions because people think they have wasted their time and energy. Which is more painful? The pain of giving up or the continued effort to succeed? There is a price for both. You must decide, are you going to pay a lot for nothing or pay a little more for success?

Included in the chapters are many stories of people who achieved beyond expectations. All of them paid a high price for success. All of them had to work at it day after day, month after month, year after year. They paid with their time, money, intellectual energy, emotional energy, and physical energy. As a result, every one of them ended up with a feeling of pride, accomplishment, and gratitude because of their efforts. That feeling is what gives it value.

~

"What truly defines us and allows us to overcome
our challenges is how we live our lives despite
the obstacles that come our way. What's truly
important is what we learn on the inside
and how we grow from our experiences."
Victoria Arlen

~

Unsuccessful Efforts Are Unavoidable!

The classic example of achieving beyond expectations is the story about Thomas Edison as he worked to invent the modern lightbulb. Sources claim Edison said, "I have not failed 10,000 times. I have not failed once. I have succeeded in proving that those 10,000 ways will not work. When I have eliminated the ways that will not work, I will find the way that will work."

Whether Edison said those words or not is unimportant here. What is important is, Edison modeled the mindset needed to make the impossible, possible. Whenever you are making a life change of any size, you will experience unmet expectations, which some people view as failures. It is unavoidable. At this point, you have a choice. You can view it as a failure, or you can view it as discovering a way it doesn't work and learn from the experience. What matters in life is not what happens, *but your reaction* to what happens!

In my research for this book, I found that everyone who achieves beyond expectations applies this positive mindset. When you are doing something you have never done before, you will experience multiple, and often gut-wrenching, unsuccessful efforts. But with this positive mindset, you will stay motivated to accomplish the task.

~

"Persistence, positivity, patience, and creativity
are essential for high achievement."
Bill Blokker, EdD

~

Persistence, Positivity, Patience, and Creativity Pay Off

Achieving beyond expectations is time consuming and often gut wrenching. The following story is an example of the most incredible accomplishments that I found in my research to illustrate the value of persistence and positivity. This inspiring story highlights Victoria Arlen, who became paralyzed and comatose. Over the next ten years, Victoria and her family experienced devastating unsuccessful events, but their collective efforts produced the most astonishing results.

It is 2005. Imagine being trapped in your 11-year-old body—paralyzed and in a vegetative state for four years—but you can hear and understand everything that is going on around you.

Doctors say you may not survive. If you do, you will never walk, talk, or function normally. You will have severe neurological deficits. So, what do you do when you hear these words? Believe them? Defy them?

Victoria Arlen was raised in a very athletic family. Ever since she was little, she had the "never give up" mindset.

After four years in her vegetative state, she was finally able to let her family know she was there. First, blinking. Then speaking. Moving one finger. Then sitting up. Finally holding her head up and eventually moving into a wheelchair. The doctors said everything she accomplished was impossible!

Even though she was wheelchair-bound, Victoria decided she could compete in swimming. She won a gold medal in the London 2012

Paralympic Games at the age of 17. She also holds swimming records in the World, American and Pan-American games.

Victoria wanted out of the wheelchair even though she was paralyzed from the waist down. She chose not to accept this situation. She was going to walk. She worked with a trainer from Project Walk. Victoria decided that walking was going to be her next gold medal!

The daily workouts were the hardest challenge of her life. She experienced no success for 14 months! She had never experienced such a challenge and such failure. She had learned from her family that when you are challenged, always dig deeper. After 14 months of failure, she experienced one small twitch in a quad muscle, nearly 10 years after becoming paralyzed. One of her favorite quotes was, "When there is a spark, fan the flame, fan the flame!" Now she was on her way. Walking. Climbing stairs. Skiing. Defying all odds!

In Victoria's words, "Blood, sweat and tears go into every victory big and small and every 'golden' moment. Challenges occur and sometimes you fall to depths that you never even knew were possible. But then with every fall you have the chance to rise higher than ever and be better than you were before. Who says you can't do the impossible? Victoria's motto: "Face it, Embrace it, Defy it, Conquer it."

Victoria says her family was the reason she surmounted all the challenges. They were the ones who would not accept the doctors' diagnoses. Her family members are her heroes. Victoria says, "Heroes in real life don't wear masks and capes. Sometimes they don't stand out at all. Real heroes can save a life or many lives just by answering the call in their heart. In the darkness of my life, when I couldn't help myself, my heroes were there… Sometimes we just need someone to lean over and whisper, 'You can do it!'"

I read Victoria Arlen's book, *Locked In* and saw a PeopleTV show "Victoria Arlen: My Miraculous Recovery." If you read her book, you will be both heart broken and delighted numerous times. To make the impossible, possible, Victoria and her family were implementing the intangibles for over ten years. Her life depended on her strong conviction to live, as well as her own and her family's courage, persistence and belief in their ability to overcome unimaginable obstacles. Victoria and her family continually achieved beyond expectations.

You Will Need Others for Support

As with Victoria and other people you will read about, there is always a team supporting the person, helping to create the exceptional achievement. The team may be formal or informal. It might consist of just two people or it could be many more. The point is, if you want to achieve beyond expectations, you will need others to support your effort.

This support can come in a variety of ways. You will need someone with the technical knowledge and skills to help you develop your talent. You will need others to provide emotional support. The size of your goal will determine the type and amount of support needed. Your success is contingent on making sure all these people have a common vision of what needs to be done to help you. They must be willing to do whatever it takes to ensure the goal is accomplished.

∽

"No matter how talented or skilled you are, you will never reach your full potential without expert guidance."
Enock Maregesi

∽

Building Your Leadership
for Team Achievement

Perhaps you are reading this book because you are in a leadership position. You might have a title (manager, director, pastor, etc.) that indicates your leadership role. Or you may not have a title, but you are still leading others.

Whichever you are, as a leader, the content of this book can assist your work. The content applies to both individuals and teams of people. Whether you are working on a personal or organization goal, you will need to learn how to inspire all team members to be as effective as possible. All team members will benefit by understanding the impact of self-awareness, emotions, habits, expectations, and self-efficacy on their performance. As a team leader, you are responsible for making that happen. The content of this book will provide you with the strategies and processes to lead your team to achieve beyond expectations.

~

"Leadership is having a compelling vision,
a comprehensive plan, relentless implementation,
and talented people working together."
Alan Mulally

~

Parents Are Leaders Too

We saw in Victoria Arlen's story how her parents and family played a critical role in her recovery. They were committed to do whatever it took to improve her situation. It took a team of people to save the life of Victoria and help her regain her physical skills. Though her father, brothers, and others played significant roles, Victoria's mother was clearly the team leader. It was "Mummy" who took the lead. She was the one who had the driving vision that Victoria could achieve whatever she wanted. She caused all the other family members, doctors, physical therapists, and others to work collaboratively to ensure her daughter's success.

The whole family had high expectations for Victoria and themselves. They believed they could help her. They had a high level of self-efficacy. They developed new habit patterns so they could efficiently care for her. Most importantly, they learned to control their emotions rather than allowing emotions to control them. The family faced a multitude of negative medical evaluations of Victoria, but they had the passion and belief that they were going to make things better for her. Together, they achieved beyond expectations.

If you have children, the most important job you have is parenting. A parent is responsible for raising children who will become contributing and responsible adults in society. Being a parent is the toughest job in the world for many reasons. Most of us are ill prepared to be parents. Many of us did not have access to a parent education program and we had to learn on our own as we went along. There was a lot of trial and error.

Even if you have access to a parenting program, it is still a daunting task. To effectively apply all the information in the parenting classes and books, you need the five intangibles. Self-awareness, emotional control, habits, expectations, and self-efficacy are foundational to your parenting efforts. The five intangibles determine how effectively you implement all you learn. Each chapter of this book will provide information about how to apply the five intangibles to your role as a parent.

~

"If there is anything we wish to change in the child, we should first examine it and see whether it is not something that could better be changed in ourselves."

C. G. Jung

~

Making Best Use of This Book

This book is designed to be used as a reference tool, recipe book, or blueprint. It is not designed to be read once in a quick fashion, then never looked at again.

As you read earlier, think of this book is an instruction manual. It offers a wealth of information and strategies on human performance and achievement. To succeed in whatever goals you have for yourself, begin the process of internalizing these important concepts and skills. Work to become consciously competent in the execution of the five intangibles. They are the foundation for all human performance.

~

"Knowledge is useless without continuous application."

Julian Hall

~

You *can* make the impossible, possible. You *can* achieve beyond expectations. All the inspirational stories in this book are there to document that it is possible to do the unimaginable. The people in these stories had to overcome huge challenges. If they can do it, *so can you!*

Key Points: Execution Transcends Talent

1. Each person has their own personal definition of what it means to achieve beyond expectations.

2. Execution transcends talent. These five intangibles are foundational to all human performance. They optimize your ability to use your talent.

   a. Self-Awareness

   b. Emotional Control

   c. Habits

   d. Expectations

   e. Self-Efficacy

3. There is a price to pay for any change you want to make. The currency of payment includes intellectual, emotional, and physical energy as well as time and money.

4. Persistence, positivity, patience, and creativity are essential. Unsuccessful efforts and obstacles are unavoidable.

5. What matters in life is not what happens, but *your reaction* to what happens!

6. Application of the content of this book will lead to greater effectiveness in your role as a leader or parent.

7. Knowledge is power, only when knowledge *is applied effectively!*

~

"Expect the best of yourself,
then do what is best to make it reality."
Ralph Marston

~

2

Self-Awareness

Eliminating Your Blind Spots

You were just diagnosed with a degenerative eye disease. The doctor has informed you that within the next year, your eyesight will be gone forever! There is no cure. You will be blind the remainder of your life. You are shocked. It takes your breath away. Then suddenly, a feeling of darkness overwhelms you.

You begin to think about the impact on your life. What will this mean? You realize you will no longer be able to see your spouse or children. Your interactions with them will be severely hindered. You think about how you will be able to hold a job. Your independence and ability to do things for yourself will be greatly reduced. All that you have planned, your life goals, will be short changed or eliminated. The impact of blindness is devastating and overwhelming. Panic and anxiety are taking over your mind.

Some people have experienced this situation. It was not a simulation; it was real. It had a dramatic impact on their lives. Loss of vision significantly handicapped their ability to function at full potential.

PEOPLE WHO have suffered vision loss often demonstrate the traits of people who achieve beyond expectations. They accept the challenges and exhibit tremendous courage and tenacity to become the best they can be, given their circumstance.

Our vision is so important to us, but we take it for granted. Are you experiencing vision impairment? This scenario was presented to get your attention. Many of us are functioning with "vision impairment," a form of blindness, even though we have full vision! We are unaware that we are experiencing this blindness. All of us experience "blind spots" when it comes to being self-aware.

What is Self-Awareness?

Self-awareness is when you become conscious about your thoughts, emotions, and behavior. Self-awareness is the foundation of all behavior. Your self-awareness alerts you to your brain/body stimulus/response mechanism. It allows you to identify all the triggers of your thoughts, emotions, and behavior. If you lack self-awareness, it is just as if you were given the diagnosis that you are blind. By fully developing your self-awareness skills you can eliminate your blind spots. Your self-awareness provides you with critical data to achieve beyond expectations.

~

"What is necessary to change a person is
to change his awareness of himself."
Abraham Maslow

~

This book is about the five intangibles that control our daily behavior. *Intangible* can be described as something unable to be touched or grasped; not having physical presence. Intangibles are "blind spots" for us because we cannot touch, grasp, or see them. To achieve beyond expectations, we must become aware of these intangibles and how they impact our daily living.

The purpose of this chapter is to stimulate your thinking about self-awareness so you can eliminate blind spots in your life. The content of this chapter is designed to inform your thinking about all aspects of your self-awareness. What is it? Why is it so important? How does it impact your life? What are strategies you can use to become more self-aware to eliminate your blind spots?

Blind is defined as unable to see; lacking the sense of sight; unwilling or unable to perceive or understand. Each of these definitions applies to our lack of self-awareness as we progress through each day.

For example, how often have you been in a conversation and people are talking over one another. No one is really listening to the others. Everyone is focused on making their own point. As a result, they do not hear or understand what others are saying. We think just because we say something, it gets heard and understood. This is a lack of self-awareness, a blind spot.

How about when you are distressed and a good friend asks you, in a caring way, "What's making you so upset?" Your tense response: "I'm not upset! Why are you saying that?" Your response indicates you are distressed, but you are unaware that you are communicating it. A blind spot.

Both examples show how people can become so focused on themselves (e.g., their own point of view or their own distress) that their self-awareness becomes clouded or non-existent about the remainder of their behavior.

You may be thinking, "This doesn't pertain to me! I'm very self-aware." That reaction is common. In fact, I often say the same thing. Then suddenly, I have an experience that jolts me and I realize I'm not as aware as I thought I was.

For example, I have an analytical, problem-solving mind that has served me well in my profession. However, when my wife or a family member tells me they are upset about something, my habitual reaction is not to recognize their hurt feelings but to immediately begin coming up with solutions to their problem. This frustrates them to no end, because they don't feel I am hearing them. They are not yet ready to discuss solutions until they can vent their negative feelings!

When they react that way, it jolts me! I realize that I am not being self-aware of what is going on around me. My subconscious habits immediately jump to problem solving. If I were more self-aware, I would spend time inquiring how they're feeling and only later, when they seem ready, begin to discuss solutions. Guess what? When I do that, it works so much better!

Self-awareness is not easy to maintain. Our blind spots are created by the intangibles because they operate at a subconscious level. Our emotions, habits, expectations, and self-efficacy limit our self-awareness.

Why is Self-Awareness so Important?

Self-awareness is the most important of the five intangibles. It is so important because it provides you with initial and ongoing insight into the workings of your emotions, thoughts, and behavior. As a result, your self-awareness stimulates your ability to monitor emotional reactions, habit patterns, impact of expectations, and your self-efficacy. Your self-awareness:

- opens your mind's eye to your unknowns;
- is the start button for expanding your capabilities;
- inspires positive response mechanisms so you can control situations or control your reactions to situations;
- provides you with feedback and data to determine what causes your success or failure;
- gives you the opportunity to pat yourself on the back when deserved or kick yourself in the butt when you need a reminder!

Self-awareness feeds your purposeful gathering of information from all aspects of your life experiences. You then can use this information to help you act in the most productive manner.

"Awareness is the power.
The greater your awareness, the greater your power."
Bryant McGill

~

What percentage of people are self-aware? Tasha Eurich, PhD, is a renowned organizational psychologist and researcher who has done extensive research on self-awareness. She reports that only 10%-15% of the people in her studies meet the criteria for self-awareness. This means that 85%-90% of people lack self-awareness about how they are functioning each day!

Furthermore, two Harvard psychologists, Matthew Killingsworth, PhD and Daniel Gilbert, PhD, revealed in a 2010 *Harvard Gazette* article that for 46% of our waking hours, we are thinking about something other than what we are supposed to be doing! We are off task for almost half of our waking time. Our mind is wandering, thinking about who knows what. This clearly means there is significant lack of self-awareness and focus!

In another study done by Green Peak Partners and Cornell University researchers, it was shown that a high level of self-awareness is the strongest predictor of success in the business world. There are hundreds of other studies and articles discussing all aspects of self-awareness and how it is critical to success in all walks of life.

Blind spots are everywhere, yet we are unaware of them. We are blind to our blind spots! This lack of awareness will significantly handicap our performance.

The importance of self-awareness cannot be understated. The more aware you are, the more likely you will achieve beyond expectations. Why? A synthesis of studies on self-awareness indicates that people who are truly self-aware:

- are more confident;
- build stronger relationships;
- communicate more effectively;
- view problems as opportunities;
- are more satisfied employees;
- use goal setting to structure their lives;
- are more proactive;
- get more promotions.

A lack of self-awareness creates problems, while a healthy dose of self-awareness builds opportunities. When you are conscious of your thoughts, capabilities, and actions you can use this information to refine your knowledge, skills, and performance. As a result, you become more competent. When you are consciously competent, you can control situations and your reaction to situations.

~

"Until you make the unconscious conscious,
it will direct your life and you will call it fate."

C.G. Jung

~

Increasing Self-Awareness Can Change Your Life

You begin to lose your hearing at two years old and are profoundly deaf by twelve. Despite what might at first seem to be a disqualifying disability, you become the first musician in history to sustain a career as a full-time solo percussionist. Dame Evelyn Glennie had a passion for music, and she would not allow her profound deafness control her ability to express herself.

Dame Glennie found herself at a young age in what's probably the worst possible position for someone who wants to be a professional musician. But she decided that not having the ability to hear didn't mean she didn't have the ability to create the music she loved.

No matter how talented a musician you are, if you can't hear your music, you must rely on execution. Glennie's self-awareness has caused her to hear music differently. During Glennie's performances, audiences see her improvising based purely on vibrations, which she feels by using her entire body, right down to her feet. Incredibly, she can perceive pitch, dynamic, tone, and rhythm with just her finely-tuned perception of vibration.

"Life is full of challenges," she says, "but we can always find alternative ways of approaching our difficulties, which often lead to new discoveries. My career and my life have been about listening in the deepest possible sense."

Through extraordinary focus and unbreakable spirit, Glennie has achieved far more than most musicians. She's received over 90 international awards for her performances, studio albums, and compositions. She played a key role in the opening ceremonies of the 2012 Olympics in London, and even performed the first-ever percussion concerto at the Royal Albert Hall in London. (Source: www.evelyn.co.uk)

Dame Evelyn Glennie had to become more self-aware. Profound deafness means you can hear absolutely nothing! How is it possible to play a musical instrument without the ability to hear? Even more amazing is the ability to play a musical instrument and be part of huge orchestra. Glennie had to invent ways of hearing. She created an entirely new self-awareness, hearing music with her body. She is truly making the impossible, possible.

Glennie had to work hard to become more self-aware so she could become consciously competent. Being *conscious* means having an *intentional awareness* of your performance: behavior, thoughts, and emotions. Being *competent* refers to the knowledge and skills you have or must develop to complete a task. When you are consciously competent, you can specifically explain what behaviors you use to cause a result and repeat those behaviors at will.

Here's an analogy. The top of a jelly jar is stuck so tight you can't get it off. A consciously competent friend tells you to hold the top of the jar under hot water for a minute. Then using a dish towel, grab on to the top and twist it off when it's still hot. The dish towel protects you from the hot top. It also gives you a better grip to turn the top. You follow the directions and it works perfectly. Your friend was consciously competent. She told you in detail what you needed to do.

Of course, that was a simple example, but the concept is true of exceptional athletes, surgeons, and electricians. They are consciously competent because they have become aware of all the behaviors, thoughts, and emotions that impact their performance. People who are consciously competent learn how to control situations and their reactions to situations.

How consciously competent are you regarding your thoughts, emotions, and behaviors? When you apply the content in this chapter, you will elevate your self-awareness and be well on your way to eliminating your blind spots.

Internal and External Self-Awareness

There are a multitude of research studies and articles on improving self-awareness. Tasha Eurich, PhD, reports there are two components to self-awareness:

1. *Internal self-awareness*: this is looking within to see how your values, passions, and aspirations impact your behavior and the actions of others.

2. *External self-awareness*: this means understanding how other people view you (i.e., seeing yourself through others' eyes).

By increasing your internal and external self-awareness, you will have an explosion of information to guide your behavior. Think about your daily life. You continually interact with others. These interactions trigger positive and negative situations. Your self-awareness regarding these situations is critical to your effectiveness. To achieve beyond expectations requires all of us to develop our internal and external self-awareness skills.

In the remainder of this chapter, we will explore multiple strategies to expand your internal and external self-awareness. As you are reading, identify the strategies you think will work best for you, given your present circumstances. At another time, if you experience different circumstances, you can return to this chapter and identify a strategy that will work in that setting.

~

"Confront the dark parts of yourself, and work to banish them with illumination and forgiveness."

August Wilson

~

Strategies to Increase Internal Self-Awareness

Life is a series of challenges. How you respond to these challenges determines the life you will have. You have the power within to control situations and to control your reaction to situations. To do this, you must increase your internal self-awareness.

Internal Self-Awareness Strategy 1: Self-Talk Awareness

All of us talk to ourselves. Sometimes it is just in our head. Other times, we vocalize our thoughts to ourselves. Your first and most important source of self-awareness is to pay attention to your self-talk: when, how, and what you say to yourself.

Your self-talk provides critical insights about your emotions and thoughts. When you focus on your self-talk, you begin to activate your ability to control your emotions, habits, expectations, and self-efficacy. For example:

- What do you tell yourself you are good at?
- What do tell yourself you can't or won't do?
- What do you say to yourself in conflict situations?
- What do you say to yourself when you face unexpected trouble?
- What do you tell yourself when you can't calm your crying child?
- What is your self-talk when you're at work?

~

"Self-talk is the window to your
inner-most thoughts and emotions."
Bill Blokker, EdD

~

There is a psychological term, "mind control." This concept has negative connotations because it is often used to refer to controlling the thinking and behavior of people, to their detriment. However, your self-talk is a form of mind control! If you tell yourself something often enough, you will believe it.

Whether you consciously pay attention to your self-talk or you don't, it still impacts your behavior. Your self-talk is continually reinforcing the beliefs you have about yourself. When words and phrases are repeated over and over, you believe them to be true.

If you continually say negative things about yourself, you will depress your productivity and ability to overcome obstacles. Worst of all, you can take on a victim mentality that causes you to think everyone is out to get you.

If you continually use positive self-talk, your productivity increases and you become a creative problem solver. Most importantly, your belief in your own ability soars. People who achieve beyond expectations have positive self-talk.

Increasing awareness of your self-talk alerts you to your personal mind control. Once you are aware of something, you can reinforce what is helping, and change what is hurting your performance. No positive changes occur in your life with a negative mindset. You must decide how you are going to talk to yourself.

~

"No positive changes occur in your
life with a negative mindset."

Bill Blokker, EdD

~

Internal Self-Awareness Strategy 2: Confirmation Bias

Dr. Peter Wason, a cognitive psychologist at University College London, first used the term "confirmation bias" to describe how people use information to support their opinions even though the information they are using is inaccurate or made up!

Confirmation bias impacts all humans in every walk of life. Here is an everyday example. You send an important text message to a person who asked you a question. You are expecting a prompt response. An hour later and you have no reply. Here are three different thoughts you may have:

1. "I knew she was going to have a hectic day. She must be swamped!"

2. "I can't believe she hasn't responded. This certainly can't be as important to her as she claims."

3. "I should have expected this. She almost never responds to my texts. I'm not important enough."

Perhaps you have had similar thoughts when people do not respond promptly to a text from you.

Now let's look a little deeper into these examples of confirmation bias:

1. "I knew she was going to have a hectic day. She must be swamped!"
   Confirmation bias: She always responds to texts. The woman amazes me with all she does. I am impressed with her capacity to get things done. She really must be dealing with a lot not to respond.

2. "I can't believe she hasn't responded. This certainly can't be as important to her as she claims."
   Confirmation bias: I have had a sense she's not really committed to this project. She and I seldom have the same priorities.

3. "I should have expected this. She almost never responds to my texts. I'm not important enough."
   Confirmation bias: I don't think much of her and I know she doesn't think much of me. Why am I surprised?

All of these can reflect confirmation bias, based on your own interpretation of the situation. Unless you confirm with the recipient why she didn't reply, you will continually be controlled by your confirmation bias, which may or not be accurate!

All humans practice confirmation bias. Business executives may practice it when looking for information to make promotions. Doctors may practice it when diagnosing patients. Police may practice it when looking for evidence to solve a crime. Parents may practice it when disciplining their children. *All* of us use confirmation bias. You cannot avoid it, so you *must be aware* that you are doing it.

~

"What the human being is best at doing
is interpreting all new information so that
their prior conclusions remain intact."

Warren Buffett

~

Confirmation bias is a form of self-deception. Whenever our brain feels challenged, it looks for support. It's a way we protect our self-esteem. We look for "evidence" that will reinforce the opinion we hold. The more strongly we feel about something, the more powerful the confirmation bias.

When a person practices self-deception, they are digging a hole around themselves. The more they practice the self-deception, the deeper the hole. It doesn't take long for the hole to get so deep they can't climb out!

How do you become more aware of and avoid the negative impact of confirmation bias? In 1985, three researchers—Charles Lord, Princeton University; Mark Lepper, Stanford University; and Elizabeth Preston, Princeton University—did a study to determine how to combat confirmation bias. The results of their study demonstrated that using the "consider the opposite" strategy effectively overcomes confirmation bias.

To successfully use their strategy, you must train your brain to be receptive of conflicting information. When you learn and activate the strategies below, your decision making will be more effective.

Use at least three of these strategies before making a judgment or decision:

1. *Increase your self-awareness.* Continuously look for examples of you using confirmation bias. Train your brain to ask yourself, "Am I using confirmation bias?" Remind yourself to use one or more of the strategies below.

2. *Remove strong emotion from the decision-making process.* Whenever strong emotion exists, your brain automatically searches for all "evidence" that you are "correct" in your thinking. Use self-talk to calm yourself. Then, in the absence of strong emotion, analyze the situation.

3. *Consider the opposite.* With this strategy, it is important to write down your thoughts. Make two lists then compare them. Identify three to five pieces of evidence or supporting information for both sides of the judgment or decision. Whenever you are forced to take an opposing view, you gain perspective. It's the philosophy of "walking a mile in the other person's shoes." Purposely identify logical and "expert-sourced" points that support one side. Then do the same for the other side. Warning: be aware that confirmation bias can impact your thinking about the "expertise" of your source. They must have extensive formal education and many years of successful experience to be an "expert."

4. *Examine your reasoning process.* It is important to write this information down. It makes it tangible. When you have concrete information, you can sort and analyze. Use these questions to guide your reasoning process:

   a. What is the expertise of my sources of information?

   b. How many reliable sources are saying similar things?

c. What reliable sources have differing information?

d. What patterns am I seeing?

e. Is what I'm thinking a realistic possibility?

By using at least three of the four strategies, it will slow down your decision-making process and help you confront your confirmation bias. As you are using these strategies, it will give your subconscious brain more information and time to process. As a result, you are more likely to avoid the negative impact of confirmation bias.

Internal Self-Awareness Strategy 3: Values and Value Conflicts

The drive to achieve beyond expectations demands a high-intensity focus and an unrelenting persistence to succeed. This passion quest can create unexpected and unintended turbulence. Value conflicts may be the source of this turmoil.

People achieving beyond expectations are continually facing forced value choices. They make decisions and take actions driven by their intensity to accomplish their goal, even to the detriment of other people or projects. However, they are often blind to this value conflict because of their intense focus on their goal. Awareness of this value conflict may occur only when they are confronted by the person or people who are experiencing the impact. This can result in an adverse situation that could escalate to emotion commotion.

A common theme of this conflict is the valuing of task accomplishment over personal relationship. Here's an example. Jennifer is driven to accomplish a specific task that will get her closer to her business goal. She is impatient and very demanding of those working with her on this task, always pushing people. The only thing that matters to her is accomplishing the task. Meanwhile, Anita experiences the brunt of Jennifer's aggressive approach when she tries to explain that the delays are due to challenges beyond their control. Jennifer blows off these explanations, so Anita feels Jennifer is disrespecting her. Jennifer has no idea Anita is experiencing this reaction. She is blind to the situation because of her intense focus on the goal. The continuance of this value conflict will have a significant negative impact on Jennifer's relationship with Anita. Jennifer must become aware of this value conflict and work to minimize it. Unwillingness to do so will sabotage her success.

～

"Self-awareness involves deep personal honesty.
It comes from asking and answering hard questions."
Stephen Covey

～

In your quest to achieve beyond expectations, are you unknowingly trampling on the internal values you hold? We experience real-life value conflicts on a regular basis. We must become aware of them to decide if we want to continue the behavior. Here are examples of real-life forced value choices. Which ones do you relate to?

Family Value Conflicts	Work Value Conflicts
• Your spouse wants to start a family but you have no desire for children at this time.	• You observe a colleague consistently bullying another colleague.
• You want to buy a house, but it means that you will have to cut back on your social and recreational activities.	• You have been sexually harassed by your supervisor, but you can't afford to lose your job if you complain.
• You are pregnant, but you can't afford another child as you are already struggling financially.	• You have evidence that your colleague is entering false data on financial reporting forms.
• You must care for your sick and aging parents who can't care for themselves, but you are so busy with your own family and work.	• A supervisor consistently takes credit for your work. He says he'll fire you if you complain to the boss.
• You were offered a promotion, but accepting it means a cross-country move that will impact your kids.	• In one-on-one conversations with you, your boss often makes racist statements about other employees.

There is no one correct answer to any of these forced value choices. To decide on any of them entails sorting through many of your claimed values. If you have already dealt with any of these issues, you know how many compromises and sacrifices you must make to get to what you think is the best answer at that moment.

The question is, are you aware of what you truly value in life? You will not really know until you experience the forced value choice head on. Talk is cheap! You can claim all kinds of values, but until you are forced to choose between two conflicting values and take a single action, you never really know.

～

"Your vision will become clear only when you
can look into your own heart. Who looks outside,
dreams; who looks inside, awakes."

C.G. Jung

～

In the early 1970s, Sidney B. Simon, Leland W. Howe, and Howard Kirschenbaum popularized the values clarification movement. They sold nearly one million copies of their first book, *Values Clarification*, in which they identified seven criteria for a value. Simon and his colleagues said for something to constitute a true value, it must meet seven criteria:

1. Chosen freely: you have ultimately chosen it yourself.
2. Chosen from among alternatives: without two or more alternatives, there is no choice and no true value.
3. Chosen after consideration of consequences: after reflection on positive and negative consequences.
4. Prized and cherished: the key is the enthusiasm associated with the value.
5. Publicly affirmed: you willingly acknowledge the value and if confronted by another person you would not deny it.
6. Acted upon: unless acted upon, it is not a value but rather a good idea or belief.
7. Part of a definite pattern of action: a single act alone does not constitute a value.

The application of these seven criteria to what you claim to value is an excellent exercise in self-awareness. When you find yourself in a forced-value choice, are you implementing these seven criteria?

Here is an example of what it may look like. Let's say your claimed value is a "healthy lifestyle."

Value Criteria	Value Example	Non-Value Example
1. **Chosen freely**	After much thought/discussion, you decide lifestyle changes are needed regarding exercise, diet, and substance use.	A doctor tells you that your excessive consumption of certain foods and alcohol is the cause of your health problems and you need to change your lifestyle. Your spouse and significant others urge you to make the changes. You say you are willing to make necessary changes but you're not happy about it.
2. **Chosen from alternatives**	You analyze multiple diet and exercise options to determine which will fit best given your lifestyle.	You make no effort to explore diet or exercise options available to you. You have no real motivation to do this. You claim you'll probably take the recommendation of the doctor.
3. **Chosen after consideration of consequences**	Your alcohol consumption provides no real value. In fact, you hate the way you feel after any amount of excessive use. You decide to stop drinking. You have found a diet and exercise program that appeals and you believe you can implement successfully.	You have taken the recommendation of the doctor with no investigation of other possible plans that may accomplish the same goals and may be more palatable to your tastes.
4. **Prized and cherished**	At present, you do not prize or cherish the way you look or feel. There are many things you would like to do but can't because of your present physical condition. The future vision of your new lifestyle is driving your decision making.	You don't really believe you have a problem. You say you have many friends doing the same things and they don't have any problems. You really enjoy the feeling you get when consuming your present diet and alcohol.
5. **Publicly affirmed**	You have established three specific lifestyle goals and have shared them with significant others and a few close friends.	You tell others you are making the changes. You give examples of how you have changed. But you are often not truthful.

Value Criteria	Value Example	Non-Value Example
6. **Acted upon**	You have a plan of action that you're implementing and documenting your activity. You have created a way to reward yourself when you hit certain benchmarks.	You follow the prescribed diet, etc., when in the presence of your spouse and significant others, but not when they are not around.
7. **Part of a definite pattern of action**	You have documentation that you have established new patterns over the past three weeks.	Sporadic changes are being implemented but you are not happy about them. There is no consistency in your efforts.

As you review this example, do you see yourself or significant others falling into either the Value Example or the Non-Value Example? It is one thing to say you value something and another to act in a conscious and consistent manner.

~

"Everything you do sends a message
about who you are and what you value."
Michael Josephson

~

Investing time using these seven values criteria to clarify your personal or company values can pay dividends. When I started my first business, I made the decision that our number one value was to provide outstanding service and products to our clients. In addition, I made the decision to create the best possible work culture for our employees and consultants. Over 30 years, we had to make many forced value choices regarding what was best for the client versus the impact on our profit margin. We always erred in favor of the customer. The same applied to our employees/consultants. Understand that there were many times when we were not happy about making these decisions. But we did it because of what we valued.

Internal Self-Awareness Strategy 4: Establishing Priorities

When asked about their work, many people respond by saying something like, "I'm overwhelmed." Or, "I'm so busy. There's just too much to do." Think about this: *Just because you are busy does not mean you are productive.*

How is it that some people don't seemed to be frazzled or overwhelmed, but they are very productive? One of the reasons is they have established priorities that drive their daily behavior.

General Dwight D. Eisenhower was a highly productive leader who was noted for getting important things done. Prior to being elected President, he was Supreme Commander of Allied Forces in Western Europe during World War II. Afterwards, Eisenhower took command of the new North Atlantic Treaty Organization (NATO) forces in Europe. He recognized that he needed a strategy to effectively establish priorities. That strategy is described below. For the purposes of this book, it has been labeled the "Eisenhower Priority Process."

Eisenhower Priority Process

To be productive in any situation, you must establish priorities. This means focusing on doing the most important tasks. This principle applies whether you are working on big comprehensive goals or performing tiny little tasks. We will always have competing priorities, so use this process to determine the order in which you will work on them.

Here is how Eisenhower established priorities. Two key terms drive the process:

1. *Important*—this designates the value of an activity. It is deemed important if it is essential to accomplish a specific goal/task.

2. *Urgent*—this is the time variable. Urgency is established by the due date of the activity. The closer the due date the more urgent.

Using these key terms, Eisenhower classified tasks he had to attend to each day into one of the following four categories:

1. **Important and Urgent = Top Priority**: This is any task that relates directly to accomplishing your goal. The due date is uncomfortably close given the work that must be done. As a result, you should focus all of your time on this task; it takes priority over all other activities. There is nothing that interferes with the accomplishment of this task. You dedicate all necessary resources to its successful completion.

2. **Important but Not Urgent = 2nd Priority**: This is a task that relates directly to accomplishing a specific goal. Given the amount of work that needs to be done, the due date is a comfortable distance away. It is secondary only to the "Important-Urgent" task. Time and resources are allocated depending on availability from the Top Priority activity.

3. **Unimportant and Urgent:** This task is unrelated to accomplishing the goals for which you are held accountable. Work on this task only when your Top

Priority and 2nd Priority are complete. The due date is rapidly approaching, but the sense of urgency for its accomplishment comes from an outside source (not you or your team). Any time or resources allocated to this activity are minimal and will occur only after your Top and 2nd Priorities are under control.

4. **Unimportant and Not Urgent:** This is a task that is unrelated to any goals for which you are responsible. The accomplishment of this task has no bearing on your work productivity. You make a conscious decision that you won't take any action on this. It is discarded.

∿

"Our greatest danger in life is in permitting
the urgent things to crowd out the important."
Charles Hummel

∿

Here's a practical example of how this Eisenhower Priority Process can be applied in real life. For many years in my professional life, I was responsible for writing proposals for our organization to obtain new contracts. If we won and got funded, a proposal might provide millions of dollars for the company. In addition to writing the proposals, I had many other leadership responsibilities.

I continually used the Eisenhower Priority Process to determine my daily work priorities. When I was working on a Top Priority project and the due date was seven days or less, nothing else was on my radar. I would beg out of meetings unrelated to the proposal. Paperwork did not get done. Phone calls and emails were not returned. I shut my phone off so I would stop being distracted by the various notifications. If I ate lunch, it was quick and at my desk.

There were even times I put a "Do Not Disturb" sign up on my desk because I didn't want people approaching me to begin a conversation. When people did interrupt me, I was polite and respectful, but they always got the message: *I can't help you now. I have a big project going and a close, close deadline.*

When I was working on a 2nd Priority project, I paid attention to some productivity disrupters. People expect emails, text messages, and phone calls returned. They want your opinion about something or just want to socialize. All these activities are disrupters to productivity if they do not relate to the project, goal, or task for which you are responsible. When I was in an "important but not urgent" situation, I usually responded to people if their queries were about work-related projects. When they were not, I would explain in a respectful manner that I had to focus on my priority items. Sometimes the explanation worked and other times it did not. Just because something is a priority for them does not mean it has to be a priority for me.

Interacting with people on the job is important though. Whenever I was in a "non-urgent" situation, I did take 10 minutes each morning, time at lunch, and 10 minutes each afternoon to interact with various people in a more social manner. However, I was always cautious. I never wanted to distract them if *they* were in an "important and urgent" mode.

∼

"We live in a time-crunched world,
and just about everything we do seems to be urgent."

Joyce Meyer

∼

As for the Unimportant-Urgent category, this effectively means that it is important to someone else, but not you. You must analyze each situation and determine how best to appease the person. I frequently had to deal with people who had urgent priorities for me, but what they wanted did not come close to being a priority for me. This was quite common with people in other departments of the company. They often thought others had to respond to their queries immediately. This did create some consternation, but I would put them off as nicely as possible. I would give them a rationale for why I had not yet gotten to what they wanted. I never was confrontational, but I always had an excuse.

The Eisenhower Priority Process is a powerful tool. Your productivity will soar and thoughts of being overwhelmed will be reduced when the Eisenhower Priority Process is applied to your daily living.

External Self-Awareness Strategy 5: Your Focus and Perspective

Tasha Eurich, PhD, told us of the importance of both internal and external self-awareness, and so far, the strategies we have covered have focused on developing your internal self-awareness. Our last two strategies will focus on external self-awareness.

Your focus and perspective control your external self-awareness. You understand situations differently depending on your mindset and where you direct your attention. Here is an activity to demonstrate how focus and perspective work together to impact your awareness.

Figure 1.

Look at the graphic in Figure 1. What do you see? Do you see a duck or a rabbit? Are you able to adjust your focus on a certain point to see a duck? Now adjust your focus to another point to see the rabbit. Move back and forth from one focus point to the other. See the rabbit, now the duck, now back to the rabbit. Focus means a point of concentration or a place to concentrate your attention or effort. When you focus on the far-left side of the graphic you see the duck's bill then the eye and head. When you focus on the far-right side of the graphic, you see the rabbit's nose, then eye and finally the ears laid back. Where you focus determines what you see. *Your focus determines your self-awareness.*

Here is an activity that will emphasize the importance of your perspective. Look at the graphic in Figure 2. What is the first thing you see? Now adjust your focus to determine what else you can see. You may need multiple focus points to see either one of the objects. Look back and forth, back and forth, from one focus point to the other. By doing this, your eyes take in different information, therefore your self-awareness changes.

Several of you are experiencing some frustration right now because you are not seeing one or both of the objects in

Figure 2. I purposely withheld information from you that would refine your focus. I did not give you a perspective.

The *Cambridge University Dictionary* defines *perspective* as "a particular way of viewing things that depends on one's experience and personality." It also means the ability to consider things in relation to one another accurately and fairly. Without a perspective you don't know what to look for. You don't know where to focus! Your brain needs more direction.

Here is some perspective; look for *words* in the graphic. Does that help? Your brain has more to work with. With the perspective of looking for words, your brain is now focusing on those shapes that represent letters. With this perspective, many of you are seeing one or two words. Now some of you are thinking, "Two words? I see one, but not two." Those of you who see two words, good for you! Just sit there with a smile on your face.

For those of you who do not see two words, focus on the white curve on the far-left of the graphic. You should see the word *OPTICAL*. Got that one? Now, focus on the dark colors starting on the far-left and move to the right. It's difficult, but you should see the letters for the word *ILLUSION*. Each of these clues gives you a bigger perspective which in turn helps you adjust your focus.

Figure 2.

Hopefully, all of you are now feeling successful. However, I know some of you are thinking, "He's really stretching it. In the word *ILLUSION*, you can barely make out the letter *I* and the two *L*s." Others of you are saying, "There's no way those white squiggles are letters!" With both words, you must stretch your perspective of letter shapes. The letter shapes are very different than what you are accustomed to seeing. *Your perspective impacts how you focus.*

In Figure 1, almost all of you were able to see the duck or rabbit or both. You read, "Do you see a duck or a rabbit?" Reading those words provided you with a perspective. Your brain was looking for characteristics of either a duck or rabbit. This gave you a mental image to aid your focus. Therefore, you looked for identifying characteristics of either a duck or rabbit. In Figure 2, I purposely did not give you any clues. You had no perspective. Your brain did not know where to focus because you had no idea what you were looking for.

Perspective and focus play an essential role in your self-awareness. In the real world, there are times when it is difficult to comprehend what others are communicating. You need perspective, then you can focus on what is being communicated.

∼

"No problem can be solved
from the same level of consciousness that created it."
Albert Einstein

∼

Here's an example. There has been a growing unease between a wife and husband. This has been going on for two days. He is on edge and irritable and she can't figure out why. There is no apparent reason. The atmosphere is getting really tense. This can't continue to go on this way.

She decides to find out what's going on. She says, "I love you very much. It really hurts to see you so upset. I want to help. Please, talk to me." He sits quietly, looking down at his hands. He slowly raises his head and there are tears in his eyes. He says, "Three days ago we talked about starting a family. You were so excited about it, and we agreed now was the time. But I'm scared to death about doing this." The wife responds, "I'm surprised because I thought you wanted a family as much as I do." He replies, "I do but I'm scared to death."

She's still puzzled. "We talked about finances and we know we can afford it," she says. "You have a great job. I don't understand what is frightening you." He sits there looking at his hands, then says, "I'm scared of being a father." She responds, "Okay, but I still don't understand. You are a great husband and I have no doubt you're going to be an amazing father." He says, "You know I never had a father. My mom was great, but I have no idea what a father is supposed to do. I'm really scared I'm going to screw it up. I'm not sure if we should have kids!"

Prior to this conversation, the wife had a problem understanding why there had been so much tension for days. Her perspective was: we are happy and we're going to start a family. With that perspective she could not focus on the source of what was bothering her husband. She continued to stay puzzled until her husband told her about his insecurities of being a father because he had no role model. Now with this new perspective, the wife can focus her conversations on relieving her husband's insecurity.

This is a similar situation as with the "optical illusion" graphic. Until you had perspective you could not see the letter shapes. Without the perspective of her husband's angst about the lack of a father role model, she could not focus on the real issue. BTW, they worked it out. They have three kids and he's a great dad!

Your external awareness is dependent on you having perspective of the other person's situation before you can focus on working to resolve whatever issues you have. This is especially critical when you're trying to resolve a conflict.

As you go about applying content from this book, how do you think you can use this information on focus and perspective? Is there a present situation where it will help? Was there one in your recent past that this info would have helped? When you become more externally aware by applying the information on focus and perspective, your interactions with others and your productivity will improve significantly.

External Self-Awareness Strategy 6: Seek Feedback from Others

This final self-awareness strategy focuses on developing your external self-awareness using a feedback process. The research on feedback is abundant. It is essential to have a candid, straight-forward sense of how others view you. Without receiving this feedback on a regular basis, you will be living a life filled with your own confirmation biases.

No matter your position in life, getting honest, straight-forward feedback from key people can improve your productivity and ability to interact effectively with others. This is true for your relationships with your significant other, with those at your work, with people at your place of worship, and elsewhere. It is true whether you are a medical practitioner, an electrician, or a cattle rancher.

~

"It takes courage...to endure the sharp pains of self-discovery rather than choose to take the dull pain of unconsciousness that would last the rest of our lives."

Marianne Williamson

~

Tasha Eurich, the organizational psychologist, tells us that when you have a high level of external self-awareness at work, you:

- are more effective in your responsibilities;
- have better workplace relationships;
- feel more satisfied.

Our perception of how others view us is of constant concern to us. Research reported in 2017 in the *Journal of Personality and Social Psychology* indicates that we enjoy relationships with others who view us in a positive manner. We like people who like us! Being aware of this mindset has an impact on your behavior and your decision making.

The report went on to say that we tend to act in the manner viewed as desirable to others, even if it is not an accurate version of who we are! In other words, what others think of us is so important that we change our behavior to be acceptable or to get approval.

At some time or another, each of us has adjusted our behavior to "get along" in the workplace and in family or social situations. Think of when you are at a social gathering. You may decide to be careful what opinions you express because you either don't want to be embarrassed or don't want to offend someone. Many people have a "rule" that they will not talk about religion or politics at family or work social events because these topics create uncomfortable situations they prefer to avoid. They stay quiet instead of speaking up and making their opinion known.

Some of you may be saying to yourself, "I don't adjust my behavior for anyone. I'm me. If people can't accept me for who I am, then it's their problem." For those of you who are thinking that way, how did you arrive at that conclusion?

When we study people who think this way, we find they have not always had those thoughts. What we know is that these people had to work hard at becoming both internally and externally self-aware. Because of this increased self-awareness, they develop the mindset that other's opinions *will not dominate* their thinking or control their behavior.

To the truly self-aware people, *other's views are weighted* depending on who the people are and the task they are trying to accomplish. Truly self-aware people are projecting their real self, most of the time. However, they have learned that given certain situations, they must make some adjustments to get the results they want. The person who says, "I'm me and I never change for anyone or anything," is a person who likely is not going to achieve beyond expectations. *Continuous high performance requires an intense focus on a goal and then constant monitoring and adjusting behavior to accomplish the goal.*

∼

"By becoming self-aware, you gain ownership
of reality; in becoming real, you become
the master of both inner and outer life."

Deepak Chopra

∼

How are you going to get the external feedback from others? Here are some thoughts to consider when asking others to give you feedback:

1. Asking for feedback, when you have never done it before, can create many negative emotions for you and the people you are asking. Avoid creating emotion commotion.

2. There are two basic questions to ask:

   a. What do I do well in my (role)?

   b. What do I need to do differently to be better at (role)?

3. When asking these questions of family or significant others:

   a. It is critical that you accept, in a non-defensive manner, whatever they say.

   b. If necessary, ask a question or two to clarify what the person has said.

4. When seeking feedback in a work setting, make every effort to get anonymous responses to any questions you ask.

5. Once you have the external feedback, analyze the information and make decisions about how you will act in the future. During this analysis process, be aware of your confirmation bias.

   a. Look for and analyze patterns. These are the true indicators of others' perceptions.

   b. What behaviors will you reinforce and continue?

   c. What behaviors will you change?

6. It is essential that the others see that you have been responsive to their feedback. You may find it helpful to point out that you are doing _____ because it was something you learned about in the feedback.

Many of you in the business world are aware of instruments available to get feedback from customers, peers, subordinates and superiors. I am not discouraging you from using these. Just be cautious that they are providing useful information. They must be *customized* for every situation. One last key point. Keep your feedback questions *simple and specific.*

~

"Self-awareness is the key to self-mastery."
Gretchen Rubin

~

Self-awareness is the most important of the five intangibles. It provides you with initial and ongoing insight into the workings of your emotions, thoughts, and behavior. As a result, you can make the adjustments so you can achieve beyond expectations.

Key Points: Self-Awareness

1. Self-awareness is the most important of the five intangibles. Self-awareness provides you with the following:

   a. Information to control the other four intangibles: emotions, habits, expectations, and self-efficacy

   b. Information to trigger the desired brain/body response so you can control situations or your reaction to situations

2. Research studies tell us self-aware people are more productive, successful, happy, and lead a fuller life.

3. Self-talk is the first and most important source of self-awareness data.

4. Confirmation bias leads to self-deception.

5. You must become aware of the value conflicts you will experience in your quest to achieve beyond expectations.

6. Use the Eisenhower Priority Process to increase your productivity.

7. Develop your external awareness by using focus and perspective.

8. Seek external feedback to increase both your effectiveness with others and your productivity.

~

"Self-awareness gives you the capacity to learn from your mistakes as well enables you to keep growing."

Lawrence Bossidy

~

3

Avoid Emotion Commotion

Tetnia is a 22-year-old single mother of three children ages three, five and six. She did not graduate from high school. She supports herself and her children by working two jobs. She cleans offices from 11:00 p.m. to 6:00 a.m. She works as a server in a restaurant from 10:00 a.m. to 2:00 p.m.

Even with the money she earns from these two jobs, she still qualifies for food stamps. She does not have a car. Tetnia's 70-year-old grandmother stays at her apartment every night to be with the children.

When Tetnia arrives home each morning, she gets the five- and six-year-old children off to school. She then takes the three-year-old to a low-income day care in a nearby church. She returns home and sleeps for an hour then heads off to the restaurant. At 2:15 p.m. she picks up the three-year-old at the day care and heads home. She does household tasks until 3:15 p.m. when she heads out with her three-year old to get her other two children at school. On the way home, when the weather is good, they stop at a park for the children to play for a few minutes.

At 5:00 p.m. they have dinner and at 6:00 p.m. grandmother arrives to care for the children and get them to bed. Tetnia goes to sleep until 9:30 p.m. She then gets ready to go to work at 11:00 p.m. Periodically, Tetnia's drug-addicted mother shows up asking for money or a place to sleep.

Tetnia was constantly in a negative emotional state. She was tired, exhausted, stressed, overwhelmed, haggard, angry. These negative emotions were controlling her life for several years. She felt like she was going crazy! She had to find a way for all this to stop. She had to find a way to dig out of this chaos for the benefit of her children. She came to realize that she could not survive and care for her children with emotional havoc controlling her life.

She started focusing on what to do to make life better. She banned all the negativity from her brain. Shortly after she started focusing on what could be, she was promoted to a supervisory position in the office cleaning job. She got a raise big enough for her to quit the restaurant job. Her next goal is to get her GED (high school diploma) and then train at a community college for a secretarial position.

TETNIA WAS living a life of daily emotion commotion. She realized that for the sake of her children it had to stop. She decided her negative mindset was destroying her life. She made a conscious decision to be positive and focus on what she could control to make life better. As a result, her life is on the upswing.

What matters in life is not what happens,
BUT YOUR REACTION to what happens.

What is Emotion Commotion?

Emotion commotion is when your life is on an emotional roller coaster. You are in continual turmoil. This emotional roller coaster is caused by the negative thoughts swirling in your head. Emotion commotion:

- encourages a downward spiral into more negativity;
- fosters failure;
- causes powerlessness;
- depresses creativity;
- impedes awareness.

Nothing positive happens in a state of emotion commotion. We must avoid emotion commotion at all cost. Your emotions will control you if you don't control them.

As discussed in chapter 1, *emotions are the most powerful* of the intangibles. You can work all you want on habits, expectations, and self-efficacy but it will do no good unless you are aware of and effectively control your emotions.

Here is the progression of events that enable you to avoid emotion commotion:

1. Self-awareness about your emotions is the critical first step.
2. Because of increased self-awareness, you can activate your frontal lobe to use emotional control skills to avoid emotion commotion.
3. Emotional stability develops when you consistently apply emotional control skills.
4. Emotional control eliminates many self-imposed barriers to your success.

This chapter provides you the information to work through this progression of events.

∽

"So, the first step in seeking happiness is learning. We first must learn how negative emotions and behaviors are harmful to us and how positive emotions are helpful."

Dalai Lama

∽

Developing Emotional Awareness

Emotion commotion disrupts all sensibilities. When your emotions take over, all logic or semblance of reality disappears. Do you remember as a young child that you would spin around and around to the point you would get so dizzy and disoriented that you couldn't walk? We do a similar thing to ourselves as adults when we let our emotions control our stability.

Let me give you a personal example of how I have let this happen to me. I would get up a 5:00 a.m. each morning and go for a five-mile run. One morning, during my run, I got to thinking about a conversation I had with my wife the day before. The more I thought about the conversation, the angrier I became. In fact, I began arguing with her in my head as I was running.

When I got home, my wife was still sleeping. I took a shower and was shaving when she walked into the bathroom. She gave me a cheery good morning and a love pat on my butt. I tore into her! I told her how ticked off I was and I really didn't want to talk. The poor woman had no idea what my problem was. She was just trying to be happy and loving first thing in the morning—and I responded with anger! Fortunately, she had excellent emotional control. She said, "Okay, let's give this about thirty minutes to calm down and then we can talk," and she left the bathroom.

Emotions had grabbed ahold of me and I was totally dizzy and disoriented. My emotion commotion was running rampant! It was like a whirlpool sucking me in. There was no escape! I had managed to create a negative emotional situation with a totally unsuspecting person! Emotion commotion can create a lot of damage to yourself and others.

How aware are you of your emotions and how they impact your thinking and behavior? Are emotions controlling your life or are you controlling your emotions? To better answer, try this Emotion Awareness Activity.

Emotion Awareness Activity

Answer the following questions in your journal or in the space provided. Your written answers provide you with a tangible and easy way to see a pattern. Seeing patterns increases your self-awareness.

1. Are you frequently anxious or nervous?
   Yes _____ No _____

2. Are you easily embarrassed? Yes _____ No _____

3. Are you frequently frustrated? Yes _____ No _____

4. Do you frequently question yourself? Yes _____ No _____

5. Do you say negative things when talking to yourself?
   Yes _____ No _____

6. Do you often procrastinate? Yes _____ No _____

7. Do you anger quickly? Yes _____ No _____

8. Do you focus on the "bad" things that can happen?
   Yes _____ No _____

9. Do you often blame others when there is a problem?
Yes _____ No _____

10. Do you frequently feel you're on an emotional high followed by an emotional low? Yes _____ No _____

How many times did you answer "Yes"? _____
How many times "No"? _____

The more times you answered "Yes," the more likely you are experiencing emotion commotion.

How Emotions Impact Your Life

Here is a list of some common and powerful emotions and their potential impact on your behavior, logical thinking, and physical health. As you read the chart, think about how you react when you experience each emotion. By doing this, you will increase your self-awareness of the impact of emotions on your life.

Emotion	Probable Causes	Potential Results
Fear	Real or imagined threat to physical or emotional safety.	Paralyzes action, weakens immune systems, facilitates depression, depresses logical thinking.
Anger	Secondary emotion—you always experience another negative emotion first, then anger.	Elevates heart rate and blood pressure, floods body with toxic hormones, inhibits cognitive functioning, may trigger verbal/physical abuse.
Resentment	Builds over time. You feel unfairly treated.	Creates deep negativity. Stress hormones saturate the body causing elevated heart rate, weakened immune system, upsets digestive system, causes recurrent negative thinking.

Emotion	Probable Causes	Potential Results
Determination	Your desire to take charge of life events. You believe you can control events or control your reaction to events.	Reduces susceptibility to negative emotions. Energizes. Inspires creative thinking. Releases endorphins. Drives goal orientation.
Enthusiasm	Excitement and positive energy to accomplish a goal. Strong positive belief in favor of something.	Increases energy for task. Releases endorphins. Energizes others. Triggers cognitive solutions.
Pride	Humble, positive reflection of success in a task or relationship.	Builds self-efficacy, releases endorphins, generates discretionary effort.
Passion	Obsessive, compelling desire for something.	Unlimited emotional and physical energy, total focus on goal achievement, self-sustaining drive for success. Generates creative problem solving.

As you can see in reviewing the potential results column of this chart, negative emotions have a toxic impact on both your intellectual and physical health. These emotions often translate into disappointing results or failure when working toward a goal. In contrast, positive emotions have a constructive impact on intellectual and physical health and significantly elevate the potential for goal achievement.

～

"Do not allow negative feelings and emotions to control your mind. Emotional harm does not come from others; it is conceived and developed within ourselves."

Carlos Slim Helú

～

Your Emotions are Self-Imposed

When you experience any life event, you have a choice as to how you will react. Two people experiencing the same event can have very different reactions. One person expresses surprise, begins to think positively, and works to make the situation better. The other person expresses dismay, continues to focus on the negatives of the situation, complaining about all the bad things that happen to him. You can choose to be either one of these people. It's up to you.

By developing an understanding of the brain's stimulus/response process, you will learn that you can control your emotions and act in the manner that is most productive for the situation.

Response to Perceived Threat

Increasing your self-awareness of how your brain functions will lay the groundwork for how you can control your emotions. Any time the brain perceives a threat, it instantly activates the fight/flight response to ensure your physical survival. For most of us in the twenty-first century, we don't need to worry about our physical survival. In our culture, we all experience things such as discrimination, disrespect, embarrassment, or criticism. Even though in most cases there is no physical survival threat, the brain still responds in the same manner as if there was that threat. It instantly activates the fight/flight mode in response to a perceived threat.

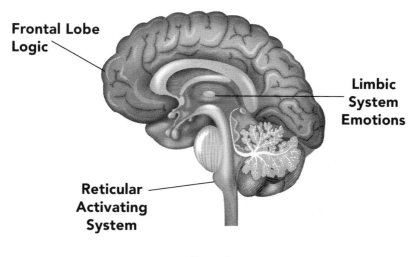

Frontal Lobe
Logic

Limbic
System
Emotions

Reticular
Activating
System

Figure 3.

Figure 3 shows the parts of your brain that play a major role in your response to a perceived threat:

- Reticular Activating System (RAS):
  o recognizes the stimulus
  o prioritizes the importance, then sends message to the limbic system
- Limbic System:
  o activates the "fight/flight response" for physical safety
- Frontal Lobe:
  o has the capacity to overrule the fight/flight response
  o provides the logic and problem solving to take control of the situation or to control your reaction to the situation

The Response to Perceived Threat diagram in Figure 4 outlines the multi-step stimulus/response process we go through that results in our behavior. When you understand this process, you:

- know how to avoid emotion commotion;
- understand that all emotions are self-imposed;
- can choose to express the emotions that are most helpful to your situation.

~

"Emotions are temporary states of mind.
Don't let them permanently destroy you!"

Anonymous

~

RESPONSE TO PERCEIVED THREAT

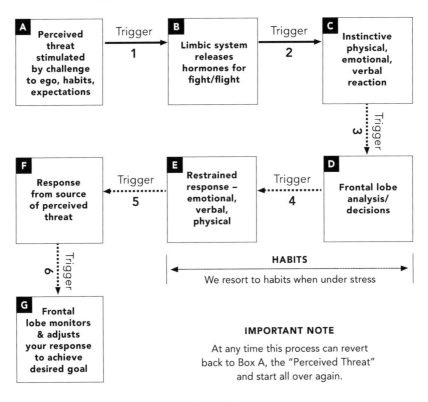

Figure 4.

ACHIEVE BEYOND EXPECTATIONS

As you will see in the diagram, there are "trigger points" for each step of the process. The *solid arrow* trigger points indicate you have *no control*. The *dotted arrow* trigger points show where *you can control* your reaction if you choose to do so. Becoming aware of these trigger points is essential to implementing your frontal lobe to control your emotions.

Here is a description of what occurs in each of the stimulus/response steps of the process. Let's imagine that you are in a meeting with several other colleagues. During this meeting, your boss negatively criticizes you for doing poor work on a project you were leading.

Response to Perceived Threat	Example
Box A—Your reticular activating system (RAS) perceives a threat. This could result from a challenge to your ego, a habitual response, or unmet expectations. **You have no control over this reaction.** This sets off Trigger 1, which stimulates Box B.	Because of the boss's criticism, you perceive a threat to your dignity.
Box B—The limbic system responds. This response is hardwired into our genetic makeup. **You have no control over this reaction.** Its purpose is to protect us in physically unsafe situations. The limbic system does not differentiate between a physical or emotional threat, so the response is to stimulate the fight/flight reaction. The limbic system sends all the signals to release hormones and prepare the body to respond. This sets off Trigger 2, which stimulates Box C.	Your lungs expand, blood pressure rises, heart rate increases, blood vessels all affected. Adrenaline, glucose, and fats are pumped throughout your body. This is followed by the release of cortisol. The body is revved up for fight/flight.

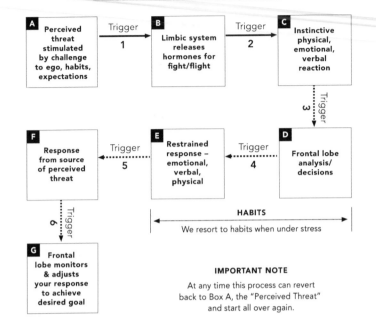

A — Perceived threat stimulated by challenge to ego, habits, expectations

Trigger 1

B — Limbic system releases hormones for fight/flight

Trigger 2

C — Instinctive physical, emotional, verbal reaction

Trigger 3

F — Response from source of perceived threat

Trigger 5

E — Restrained response – emotional, verbal, physical

Trigger 4

D — Frontal lobe analysis/decisions

Trigger 6

G — Frontal lobe monitors & adjusts your response to achieve desired goal

HABITS
We resort to habits when under stress

IMPORTANT NOTE
At any time this process can revert back to Box A, the "Perceived Threat" and start all over again.

Response to Perceived Threat	Example
Box C–You have an instinctive initial physical and emotional reaction. You have no control over this reaction. You recognize this by the sensations in your body and perhaps a physical or verbal response. This sets off Trigger 3, which stimulates Box D. .	Your chest starts pounding and face begins to feel warm and turns a little red. Your mouth begins to feel dry. You are embarrassed and then intimidated. You have trouble making eye contact with the boss. Your muscles start to tighten. You say to yourself, "What's this all about?"
Box D–**This is where you can take control of your response.** You activate the frontal lobe to analyze all the data you have (past experiences, present situation, future goals) to decide how you will respond given all the variables of the situation. This analysis takes place in micro-seconds of time. Much of the analysis is done subconsciously. This sets off Trigger 4, which stimulates Box E. It is important to note that your *habits* play a major role in determining your behavior here. You must become aware of this and decide if your habits are helping or hindering the situation.	Multiple thoughts race through your head. First you are surprised and embarrassed. You thought you had done a good job on this project. You're wondering what your coworkers are thinking. Now you're getting irritated. You're trying to decide how best to act. Should you come back strong and defend yourself? Should you sit and take it and talk to the boss later? The one thing you know for sure is, you do not understand why the boss is so upset.

Response to Perceived Threat	Example
Box E–**You are in control of how you respond.** You respond with a statement/ action that you think will best deal with the perceived threat and the goal you want to accomplish. You are working to control your body language and tone of voice to be consistent with the message you want to send verbally. Your response sets off Trigger 5, which stimulates Box F. It is important to note that *habits* play a major role in your behavior here.	When the boss finally stops talking, you take a deep breath and say, "I am sorry I did not meet your expectations. I thought I had done what we talked about. I would like to meet with you later today or tomorrow to clarify your concerns then make the necessary changes."
Box F–The other person responds. **You have no control here**. The perceived threat (person) will respond in a manner that best serves her/his purpose. This person's response sets off Trigger 6, which stimulates Box G.	The boss responds with another negative statement but closes by saying you should schedule an appointment with the secretary.
Box G–**You are in control here.** You analyze the response of the perceived threat. Is it getting worse? Staying the same? Calming down? You are back to analyzing your options to respond so you get the results to achieve your goal. You decide and act. **You must continue to monitor and adjust.**	You're still irritated with the boss. You can't understand what is going on in his head. Why is he attacking you? You thought you had done a great job! You are relieved he is backing off. You want to calm this situation down. Your response is to nod your head and say, "Will do."

～

"The sign of intelligent people is their ability to control emotions by the application of reason."

Marya Mannes

～

This example is a positive demonstration of the process by which people respond to a perceived threat. In this example, there was "resolution," to some degree, in a short amount of time. Many situations in the real world are not so easily resolved. However, the important point to

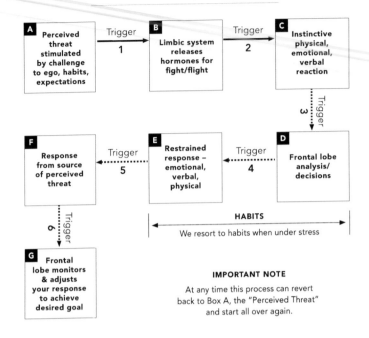

understand is that you can control situations, or you can control your reaction to a situation at several stages of the process. Let's go back and examine exactly where you can take control of your emotions.

As the graphic shows, Boxes A, B, and C happen automatically and you cannot control them. However, you have an opportunity to control Boxes D, E, and G. You learn to control them by increasing your self-awareness about what is triggering your behavior and then activating your frontal lobe to control your verbal and non-verbal behavior.

Depending on the effectiveness of your emotional control and the response of others in the challenging situation, the emotional energy can get better or worse. If you always believe you are in charge, you will never feel like the victim with no control! With this mindset, you can create the options that eventually lead to a satisfactory conclusion. If you cannot control your emotion commotion, it is likely you will find yourself back to Box A. In other words, by allowing emotion commotion, you will be re-triggering the perception of a threat and the fight/flight response. This results in a circular battle with a more toxic atmosphere.

All emotions are self-imposed. You can control situations or control your reactions to situations when you choose to do it. You now have the knowledge to begin training your brain so you can take control to achieve beyond expectations.

~

"The true mark of maturity is when somebody
hurts you and you try to understand their
situation instead of trying to hurt them back."
Anonymous

~

How will you apply the Response to Perceived Threat process in your daily living? Knowledge is power only when it gets applied. To stimulate your thinking, here are three thoughts to consider. Writing your responses to each in your journal will help you apply this information.

- What are two important things your learned from the Response to Perceived Threat description?

- Identify some examples of actions that trigger your emotion commotion.

- Identify some examples of behavior you can use to prevent emotion commotion when you recognize these triggers.

Learning to Train Your Frontal Lobe

We all have the capacity to train our frontal lobe to take charge during the Response to Perceived Threat process. You first must train your reticular activating system to alert you to the triggers. Then you must train your frontal lobe and limbic system to work together to control your emotions and act out of logic rather than emotion.

Your reticular activating system is hardwired to filter and prioritize all sensory information. It has three primary functions:

1. Safety—ensure your physical and emotional safety

2. Efficiency—stimulate development of habit patterns that cause you to function with automaticity

3. Goal Orientation—causes you to focus on those stimuli that will help you accomplish your goals

Your RAS alerts you automatically as described in the Response to Perceived Threat graphic. It functions in the priority order just described. The most important point to understand is that, once you safeguard your personal safety, you can program your RAS to perform the way that best serves your goals. This programing occurs when you consciously activate your frontal lobe to direct the RAS.

When trained, your RAS and frontal lobe will work together to establish emotional reactions and habits that are productive to accomplish your goals. Just like the development of any other skill or behavior, this training takes time and effort.

Five-Step Emotion Control Process

Once you become aware of the triggers in the Response to Perceived Threat, you can begin to successfully control your emotions.

You must use your frontal lobe to become aware of how you habitually respond during turbulent times. If your habitual emotional responses are productive, tell yourself you're doing a good job and reinforce your habits. If your habitual emotional responses don't get the results you desire, you must begin to establish new habit patterns.

The purpose of the Five-Step Emotion Control Process is to train your brain to develop the habit patterns needed to implement an effective Response to Perceived Threat and avoid emotion commotion.

The Five-Step Emotion Control Process prompts self-awareness of your habits in stressful situations. The five-step process can be accomplished in less than 10 seconds. It guides your use of the frontal lobe. It gives you the opportunity to develop new habit patterns if you so choose. Use these self-talk key words to prompt your behavior:

1. Trigger
2. Pause—Think
3. Act
4. Monitor
5. Adjust

∼

"Positive thinking will let you do everything
better *than negative thinking will.*"
Zig Ziglar

∼

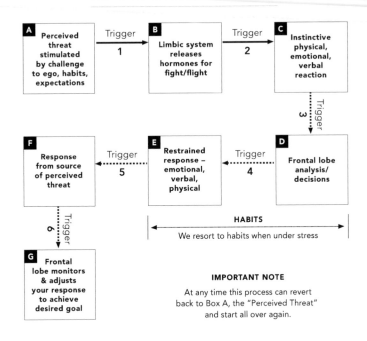

Five-Step Emotion Control Process

1. *Awareness of trigger*: This is Box C in the Response to Perceived Threat—your instinctive physical, emotional, verbal reaction. You experience the initial emotional discomfort—confusion, frustration, worry, disbelief. This is the time you *must* activate your frontal lobe to take control.

2. *Pause*: This is Box D—frontal lobe stops all verbal reactions and body language. Here is where you may have to fight to push down your initial habitual response.

   a. *Use self-talk*: force and encourage your frontal lobe into action. Use positive and purposeful words to drive your behavior.

b. *Remove your ego*: demand your frontal lobe control your limbic system and ego. Stop the fight/flight thinking. Use logic to determine what is best to improve this situation for both short and long term.

c. *Think*: give the frontal lobe time to think. What is the best result I can get in this situation? What behavior is going to get me the results I want?

d. *Decide*: force your frontal lobe into action. You have monitored and now you are going to adjust your behavior to get the best results for this situation.

3. *Act*: This is Box E—be confident, positive and purposeful. You are now acting out of logic rather than emotion. You can succeed.

4. *Monitor*: This is Box F—your frontal lobe activates your external self-awareness to determine how your words and actions impact the others.

5. *Adjust:* This is Box G—your frontal lobe uses self-awareness data to determine what you need to do/say to keep moving forward on a positive course.

As with mastering any skill, continuous practice is necessary. Through coaching and practice, you get better at monitoring and adjusting your thinking and behavior to ensure you're having the desired results. This process will develop "automaticity" with these complex emotional skills. Expect that there will be ups and downs in this learning process because the learning process is one of trial and error.

Your ability to consistently control your emotions is dependent on these six variables:

1. The developmental level of your frontal lobe

2. The knowledge, skill, and training you have had regarding using your frontal lobe to control your emotions

3. Use of the process of visualization to mentally rehearse the emotional skills you want to develop (See page 177 for a complete description of visualization.)

4. Use of self-talk to cue the emotional skills and processes you want to develop

5. Emotional control skills modeled by significant others in your life

6. Your motivation to use emotional control skills to avoid emotion commotion

~

"75% of careers are derailed for reasons related to emotional competencies, including inability to handle interpersonal problems."
Center for Creative Leadership

~

Concerning the development of your frontal lobe, Professor Sarah-Jayne Blakemore, a neuroscientist with the Institute of Cognitive Neuroscience at University College London tells us that researchers have discovered that the frontal lobe is still developing until people reach their mid-30s!

This is important information. Until the frontal lobe is fully developed, you cannot expect to consistently control your emotional responses. "Consistently" being the key word.

It is unrealistic to expect any *consistent emotional control* from children before they reach age 12. They don't have the developmental capacity to consistently control their emotional reactions. Teens can be taught emotional control skills and can use them with sporadic effectiveness. Teenagers have greater success when they have significant adults in their lives modeling effective use of emotional control skills and providing them coaching and positive support.

~

"Emotional intelligence begins to develop in the earliest years. All the small exchanges children have with their parents, teachers, and with each other carry emotional messages."
Daniel Goleman

~

For people in their 20s to mid-30s, the frontal lobe is nearing full development. With proper modeling behavior, knowledge, skill development, and positive coaching, they can demonstrate generally consistent emotional control. During trying times, they may struggle with emotions, but with typical day-to-day challenges, they should have good results.

To develop emotional control skills, you must experience turbulent times. The development of emotional control skills does not occur during calm and pleasant situations. It is during challenging situations that you learn how to recognize triggers and how to activate your frontal lobe to take control. This is where coaching and modeling behavior play a significant role. When you have a person who can help you monitor a reaction, it provides you with valuable information to adjust your behavior.

~

"Embrace your problems.
They are the source of your strengths!"
Bill Blokker, EdD

~

Controlling Common Negative Emotions

Researchers have identified hundreds of human emotions. There are four powerful negative emotions that paralyze performance. Each of these have related emotions that cause similar problems. It is most important for you to become aware of how these negative emotions immobilize your brain and body functions. Then learn how to control them so you can achieve beyond expectations.

- Fear—anxious, intimidated, vulnerable, insecure
- Anger—irritated, aggravated, frustrated
- Exhaustion—worn out, drained, tired
- Overwhelmed—helpless, inadequate, inferior

Fear–Anxious, Intimidated, Vulnerable, Insecure

Fear and the related emotions are at the top of the list of negative emotions that paralyze achievement. Fear of failure occurs because people believe they have little or no control of a situation.

For the sake of this discussion, we exclude fear related to physically violent acts. Our focus is on fear generated by your own thinking regarding various daily activities at home, work, or in society.

If your fear becomes uncontrollable, it can transform into a phobia, a type of anxiety disorder stemming from a highly irrational fear of an object or situation. Reactions triggered by phobias may be extreme. People suffering from phobias should seek professional advice.

Fear and the associated emotions come about because you think you do not have power in a given situation. The "lack of power" mindset is often generated by the beliefs you have about yourself. When you feel powerless, you:

- think you don't have the knowledge/skills to perform at the desired level;
- are focused on the negative consequences of action that generate emotion commotion.

～

"Courage is resistance to fear,
mastery of fear, not absence of fear."

Mark Twain

～

How do you overcome the "lack of power" mindset? There are multiple ways. For this section we are going to focus on one that deals with overcoming fear.

Fear Awareness Activity

To conquer fear, you must face it head-on. You must educate yourself about all aspects of the fear. In your journal, write down your answers to the following questions. By writing your answers, it makes your thoughts "real." When they are real, they are easier to understand, analyze, and manage.

Think about a goal, decision or action you are considering. Keep that in mind as you progress through this activity.

1. Fear is generated by people focusing on potential negative consequences rather than the positive consequences of an action or decision.

    a. Make a list of all the negative consequences of what you want to do.

    b. Make a list of all the positive consequences of what you want to do.

    c. Share your list with a variety of other people. Find out which of the items on each list are logical and are likely to occur.

2. Fear is triggered because people think they can't control the results.

    a. What are things you think you can't control?

    b. Do you think you lack knowledge/skill to do what you want to do?

    c. What help from others might be needed for you to feel more in control?

    d. What resources do you need to be more secure?

3. Ask yourself, are other people doing what you are afraid of doing?

    a. Can you talk to them about your fears? If so, do it. Find out what these people do to succeed and overcome their fears.

    b. If you can't talk with them, do online research about how these people were able to succeed.

Summarize all that you have written above. What insights have you gained? What thoughts and actions are you going to take to minimize your fear? You are in control.

You can focus on the negatives or the positives. Which will serve your better?

Because of doing this activity, many people discover there is no real basis for their fear. They learn many other people have succeeded in similar situations. They see that their fear is self-imposed. Use your frontal lobe to overcome your "**FEAR**—**F**alse **E**vidence **A**ppearing **R**eal!"

Anger–Irritated, Aggravated, Frustrated

What is anger? Where does it come from? What is the impact of anger?

Anger is a common negative emotion that is misunderstood by many of us. The emotions *irritated*, *aggravated*, and *frustrated* are included in this category because they are varying degrees of anger.

Anger is a secondary emotion. Prior to getting angry, people first experience one or more negative emotions. This emotion commotion escalates until they explode into anger. The purpose of anger is to regain power or dignity by striking back or overwhelming your opponent! In effect, the exact opposite happens. When someone else pushes you to the point of anger, you have lost control and they are in control!

> **Anger is a secondary emotion.**
> **Anger is a cry for help!**

Here is a most important point. Anger is detrimental to your health. Anger is toxic. Anger is a corrosive. When you get angry, you are forever damaged in some way from the self-imposed toxic burn. Is this what you want to do to yourself? Do you want to deal with the pain and agony of a toxic burn? You decide if you are going to pay attention to the danger signals leading up to the toxic spill. Once the corrosive poison spills over, it runs rampant, devouring everything around it.

Consider also how your anger impacts others, especially those to whom the anger is directed. There is no doubt that anger is contagious. When you get angry with someone, they often feel threatened or disrespected. To save face, to protect their ego, to regain control, they strike back with anger.

During angry outbursts, people say hateful things. It is not unusual for angry people to be unaware of what they say or do during the height of anger—and the situation worsens. Some people become physically violent. Negative emotions and corrosive toxins devour all they touch. Then the entire situation deteriorates! Now the toxins are spilling over from two people.

Anger creates many problems and solves nothing! You may disagree with this last sentence because you think anger is sometimes useful. For instance, you may have thoughts like, "I got angry with my sister. It solved my problem. I told that !#@* just what I thought. She'll think twice before messing with me again."

Let's analyze that thinking. Because of your angry outburst at your sister, her ego is threatened. She feels disrespected. She feels challenged. There are three options she can choose from when angry. She can choose to 1) fight, 2) flee, or 3) go with the flow. If she is emotionally *unstable*, she is going to choose to fight! She will retaliate to gain control to make herself feel better. If this happens, there are now two toxic spills!

If she is emotionally *stable,* she will use her frontal lobe to control her reaction and decide on her next steps. She can flee or go with the flow, but neither will spill more toxins. For instance, she may suggest taking a break and coming back to the topic of disagreement the next day (flee). Or she may ask you to tell her more about why you are so upset, then listen to you and acknowledge your feelings (go with the flow). Emotionally stable people use their frontal lobe to control their emotions and do nothing to escalate the negative emotions of others.

Anger Awareness Activity

If you still think anger can be productive, let's look back at times you got angry. It's important to become self-aware of your thoughts and emotions. In your journal, answer these questions:

- What thoughts and emotions were you experiencing prior to experiencing anger? (situation, emotions, behavior)
- What followed when one or both parties got angry? (emotions, behavior)
- What was the original objective you wanted to achieve before you got angry? (Solve a problem? Protect your ego?)
- Did the anger help accomplish your original objective?
- Were things better or worse because of the angry outburst?

If your honest analysis of the situation tells you good things came from your angry outburst, you have experienced a very unusual result. Seldom does anger result in a mutually agreeable ending.

~

"Anger is toxic. Anger corrodes the
vessel in which it is held."

Bill Blokker, EdD

~

Anger is a secondary emotion. You experience other negative emotions before you become angry. Anger can be controlled when you become aware of these signals. When you become aware of the signals that precede your anger, you can devise how you are going to adjust to the situation. You always have multiple options. You can flee, fight, or go with the flow!

With this analysis, you may realize that it is best to change your immediate objective. You may recognize the most important immediate goal is to calm the situation. If that's the case, you can flee or just go with the flow. If your objective is to be strong and maintain your position, then you will probably fight!

Whichever your choice, remember that *you are in charge of you!* You can decide how you will act in each situation according to the objective you are trying to accomplish.

~

"It is wise to direct your anger towards problems—
not people; to focus your energies
on answers—not excuses."

William Arthur Ward

~

Become aware of the emotions before the anger, then use your frontal lobe to control your emotions and redirect your behavior. Quick fixes seldom occur. As is the case when learning any new skills, expect that learning to control anger will be a challenging and time-consuming process. You're developing new habit patterns and this is a time-consuming process. It is important you do this for both your physical and emotional health.

Exhausted - Worn Out, Drained, Tired

I'm exhausted. I'm worn out. I'm drained. I'm tired. How often do you hear these words coming out of your mouth? Do you even recognize that you are saying them?

Saying them can be habitual. As with any habit, you don't know you are doing it. Whether you say the words out loud or internally in your mind, they impact your ability to achieve beyond expectations. By saying such words, you are speaking into existence your *inability* to accomplish something. You are talking yourself into being incapable of pushing forward because you lack the physical or mental energy. You are slamming on your brakes!

When you say you are exhausted, it seldom means you are physically unable to continue an activity. Rather, it means you are intellectually or emotionally strained. You want to stop what you are doing but you need to have an excuse to do so.

Saying you are exhausted, worn out, drained, or tired is a way to stroke your ego. You are telling yourself how hard you have worked and want to feel good about it. You want others to know the effort you put forth, so you tell them how exhausted you are.

The fact is, humans have far, far more physical, intellectual, and emotional capacity than we realize. Consider these examples:

- How would you like to walk 930 miles across Antarctica in 54 days pulling a 400-pound sled in sub-zero weather? That is over 17 miles per day! Colin O'Brady did this from November to December, 2018.

- How about Aron Ralston, amputating his own forearm, repelling down a 65' cliff using one arm, then hiking seven miles back to civilization?

- How about Charlotte Heffelmire, a 19-year-old girl, who lifted a two ton burning pickup truck off her father?

These are amazing feats that demonstrate we have no idea of our true capabilities until presented with the opportunity to excel at something that seemed impossible. The reason there are so many vignettes in this book about people achieving beyond expectations is to create your awareness of what is possible.

The Navy Seals are the epitome of making the impossible, possible. They are guided by what they call their "40% Rule"—when you think you are intellectually, emotionally, or physically exhausted and believe you can do no more, you are operating at only 40% of your total capacity. Their unbelievably rigorous training is designed to create the belief that exhaustion is just a state of mind. When they think they are exhausted, they really have 60% more capacity to accomplish their task!

Exhaustion is a self-imposed emotion. You convince yourself that you are tired and can do no more. It becomes a self-imposed emotional barrier. In reality, you have far more physical, intellectual and emotional capacity. You just choose not to use it.

The key to avoiding exhaustion is to maintain a positive mindset and self-talk because negativity provokes more negativity! It sends your body a message to release hormones that make you tired. It creates a downward spiral of negative body chemistry and thinking that leads to greater exhaustion.

A positive mindset and self-talk have the opposite effect. They send messages to your brain to release hormones that will provide energy and take away pain. Positive self-talk allows your brain to work in a creative manner. Positive mindset causes your brain and body to overrule the exhaustion. When you choose to use positive self-talk, your capacity increases exponentially.

~

"Exhausted people focus on the strain of the past.
Energetic people focus on the joy of the future."
Bill Blokker, EdD

~

Overwhelmed - Helpless, Inadequate, Inferior

All of us have felt overwhelmed at times in our lives. It is a common emotion. When you ask people why they feel overwhelmed, helpless, inadequate, or inferior, they may cite reasons such as these:

- My problem is just so complicated.
- There's no time to do it all.
- I've got 14 gazillion things I'm supposed to do.
- I don't have a clue what to do or where to begin.
- Problems are coming at me from all directions.
- I've got to solve everybody else's problems.

- The pressure never stops. It is continuous day after day.

- This project is gigantic. I've never had to deal with anything so big.

Whatever your reasons for being overwhelmed, you need self-awareness about this emotion to determine what you can do to control it. As with all of our emotions, you have a choice. You can either be controlled by emotion commotion or you can choose to control it.

Even people with emotional control can think they are overwhelmed, but what they have learned is to pay attention to their self-talk. What they tell themselves helps identify the source of the emotion and potential solutions. Here are some examples of what emotionally stable people might say to themselves and the actions/solutions on which they focus to reduce the thoughts of being overwhelmed.

Self-Talk Triggers of Feeling Overwhelmed	Actions/ Solutions
"My emotions are overwhelming me."	Pause. Step back. What is triggering the emotional deluge? What do I need to sort through what is real and made up?
"I've never had a project this big. This is huge and complex."	Break it down into manageable pieces. Incremental goals. Establish priorities. Start small.
"Crap! This deadline is crazy. No way can I get it done on time."	What are the priorities? What quality is needed? Can I get some help? How do I get the deadline extended? What is the best I can do given time constraints?
"Why am I doing this? It makes no sense. There are more important things to do."	How important is this to my job or life? How do I get the boss to re-arrange the priorities? What if I do _____ first then do _____?

Self-Talk Triggers of Feeling Overwhelmed	Actions/ Solutions
"I don't have a freaking clue how to do this!"	What can I get done with the knowledge/skills I have? What knowledge/skills do I need to develop? Who can help me with this?
"This is crap! I want no part of this. Why me?"	If I don't do this, what will happen? How important is this to my job/life? Can I get someone else to do it?

Your negative self-talk must serve as a trigger to alert your frontal lobe to take charge. By monitoring your self-talk, you can adjust your thinking and change your behavior to make the best of a difficult situation.

One of the reasons people say they are overwhelmed is they have multiple demands on their life that all appear to need simultaneous action. It's like trying to juggle 10 balls at once. Establishing priorities is essential to eliminate this thinking.

Recall the information in chapter 2, where the Eisenhower Priority Process was presented (page 57). Whenever you apply this method, it clarifies what is both important and urgent. This allows you to focus both your intellectual and emotional energy on one thing at a time. By having a clear focus and a plan of action, you eliminate the overwhelmed emotion.

Stress in Your Life–Eustress or Distress?

People often say they are experiencing stress in their life. It can arise from family issues, parenting, finances, religion, work, or many other factors. In fact, some people wear their high stress level as a badge of honor. When they are asked how they are doing, the common answer is, "Really stressed out! Got so much going on."

All stress is self-imposed. You determine a situation is negative and that initiates emotion commotion. Or you determine a situation is positive and you choose to be constructive about it. It depends on how you interpret the stress you feel. If you interpret the stress in a NEGATIVE way, it is DISTRESS. If you interpret the stress in a POSITIVE way it is EUSTRESS (pronounced *yoo-stres*).

What matters in life is not what happens,
but YOUR REACTION to what happens!

What factors stimulate distress versus eustress? Here are some of the causes.

Causes of Distress and Eustress

Distress results from:	Eustress results from:
• lack of knowledge or skill	• being consciously competent
• negative environments	• positive, supportive environments
• being unfocused	• being goal focused
• negative interpretation of an event	• positive interpretation of an event
• doubt in your ability to succeed	• belief in your abilities
• procrastinating	• being action oriented
• undisciplined time management	• effective time management
• unmet expectations	• managing expectations

Both distress and eustress have an impact on your mind and body. Distress causes your body to release toxins that result in all types of negative reactions. Eustress stimulates positive hormones and energy to allow you to achieve beyond expectations.

Impact of Distress and Eustress

Distress	Eustress
• retards physical, emotional, and intellectual performance • leads to physical or mental illness • fosters negative self-talk • stimulates negative feelings • breeds failure	• empowers physical, emotional, and intellectual performance • facilitates good mental and physical health • fosters positive self-talk • stimulates positive feelings • generates success

Significant research indicates distress is a contributing factor to many health issues such as cancer, liver disease, suicide, lung disease, motor vehicle accidents, heart attacks, and high blood pressure. The more you choose to feel distress, the more likely you will become physically ill or worse!

~

"Don't let your mind bully your body into believing
it must carry the burden of its worries."

Astrid Alauda

~

When experiencing a turbulent situation, you choose how you react. Your choice can lead to either distress or eustress. Perspective—how you interpret your experience—is the key. Two people experiencing the same life event can interpret it in very different ways. Here are life events many of us have experienced:

- death of family member/spouse
- birth of a child
- marriage
- divorce
- hospitalization, surgery
- abuse—physical, sexual, mental
- new job
- loss of a job
- starting college
- graduating from college
- buying/selling a house
- moving to a new city
- retiring
- holiday seasons

You can interpret life events in either a positive or negative manner, causing either eustress or distress. Here are two examples:

Shaun T is an international fitness expert and motivational consultant. He was sexually abused for five years as a preteen. As you can imagine this resulted in a roller coaster of negative emotions which impacted his life for many years. When he was 13 years old, Shaun made the decision he was going to take charge of his life. He was no longer going to be a victim, controlled by negative emotions. Because of his positive mindset, he turned the traumatic experiences into a positive driving force. It has been a long and arduous journey for him, but he has maintained his positive outlook and as a result, achieved beyond expectations. Shaun learned that he could not continue living a life of distress because of his awful experience. He took control of his emotions and turned the distress into eustress.

What Shaun T did was not easy or a quick fix. He had to work at it for many years. In fact, he will tell you that he still must deal with remnants of that negative experience today. Most importantly, Shaun learned that a negative situation can be overcome by a trust and belief in your ability to remain positive and look at every challenge as an opportunity to grow.

In January 2017, Serena Williams, the #1 ranked women's tennis player in the world, won the Australian Open while three months pregnant. After missing 18 months on the professional tennis tour because of the pregnancy and giving birth to her daughter, she entered the French Open. This was her first significant tournament since giving birth. Serena won her first match. In the second match, she was losing badly. She lost the first set and was down two games to nothing in the second set.

This is the time when many players would begin to feel significant distress. If she lost the second set, she would be eliminated from the tournament. When she lost the second game in the set, Serena let loose with a primal scream. The entire stadium was shocked. To Serena, it was her message to herself to turn the distress into eustress.

Serena Williams is the most highly-skilled and knowledgeable tennis player in the world. She knew she could win if she got control of her emotions. The primal scream threw a switch in her mind and body. She was going to take control both emotionally and physically. From that point on she played amazing tennis. She won the match.

When interviewed after the match, Serena was asked about the scream. She said it was her way of taking her frustration concerning her poor play and turning into a positive situation. Throughout the rest of the tournament, television commentators were comparing Serena's response to other players' reactions. When not doing well, other players would usually go into distress, getting angry with themselves and focusing on the negative. As a result, their performance suffered.

Stress is neutral and self-imposed. We choose to create distress or eustress. People who achieve beyond expectations know how to monitor and adjust their thinking to turn potential distress into eustress. You decide. You are in charge of how you think and how you interpret what is happening around you. Are you going to cause yourself to feel eustress or distress?

For example, during the end-of-year holiday season, how do you react? Some people continually worry and become negative about all the things they need to do to ensure a great celebration. Others are euphoric and enjoy every aspect of the activities during the season.

Similarly, new college students and new employees in a job often experience significant distress worrying about how they will be able to function in a new situation. Others experience eustress, looking forward, with anticipation to the new and challenging experiences they will have.

～

"All stress is self-imposed.
You decide if it's distress or eustress."
Bill Blokker, EdD

～

When people must face a significant negative event such as death, divorce, financial difficulties, or unwanted pregnancy, they experience grief and stress. There is no intent here to minimize the emotions or significance of any of these negative life events. Grieving in any manner is important, necessary, and takes time. Grieving also creates stress.

Many people who have experienced one of these significant negative situations will tell you it is a blessing in disguise! When they say that, they are choosing to focus on the positive aspect of the difficulty. This does not minimize the severity of the situation. The mindset of this person is, I am choosing to focus on any positive I can find because I know that focusing on the negatives will only increase my grief.

Pay attention to your self-talk in difficult situations. Your self-talk tells you how you're interpreting the situation. With this awareness, you can then decide to experience distress or eustress. Think back to the Response to Perceived Threat graphic and explanation (page 80). Immediately after your "instinctive emotional/physical reaction" you have your first opportunity to use your frontal lobe and take charge of your emotions. Your self-talk acts like a GPS guiding you to the path best to follow. Choose to focus on the positive. Decide what is best for you and then go about acting on it.

Emotional Control as a Learned Skill

Remember that using your frontal lobe to take charge of your emotions is a learned skill. Developing emotional control skills takes effort and time. If you choose not to develop them, you will remain mired in emotion commotion or worse. Is that what you want?

Remember, the most valuable things we have in life are hard earned. Accept the challenge of learning how to use your frontal lobe to control your emotions and you will be become unstoppable!

∼

"When we long for life without difficulties,
remind us that oaks grow strong in contrary winds
and diamonds are made under pressure."
Peter Marshall

∼

Key Points: Avoid Emotion Commotion

1. Emotions are the most powerful of the five intangibles.

2. Emotion commotion breeds negativity and toxicity.

3. Negative emotions foster all types of physical and emotional illnesses and paralyze performance.

4. Positive emotions stimulate good health, creativity, and productivity.

5. In all challenging situations, you have a choice of how you act on your emotions.

6. Use the Response to Perceived Threat process to understand when and how you can control your emotions.

7. Use self-talk and body reactions to trigger your awareness of potential emotion commotion.

8. Activate your frontal lobe to control your emotions.

9. All emotions, whether positive or negative, are self-imposed.

∼

"You can conquer any negative emotion.
You created them. You can control them!"

Bill Blokker, EdD

∼

4

Habits
Your Hidden Mind Chains

The elephant is the world's largest land mammal, standing 8'–13" tall and weighing 5,000–14,000 pounds. Elephants are extremely powerful animals. For centuries they were used as beasts of burden; they can pick up 600–1,000 pounds and pull as much as nine tons. In addition, elephants are known as one of the most intelligent animals. There are reports that they understand human body language, show empathy, and have extraordinary memories.

Given their size, power, and intellect, it is shocking that an elephant chained to a small wooden stake in the ground does not try to pull itself free. Why is this? They should have no trouble recognizing they can easily free themselves and move wherever they want. But they don't!

The reason, when very young, they are chained to a steel ring embedded in concrete. No matter how hard they pull, they cannot free themselves. Day after day they attempt to pull free, but without success. Eventually, they learn to walk to the end of the chain and stop. They no longer pull and tug to free themselves.

Once this pattern is established in the elephant's mind, it can be chained to a small wooden stake that can easily be broken, or pulled out, but the elephant does not try. The elephant is now held by its hidden mind chain!

What are your hidden mind chains? What limits have you established to your power, strength, and intellect that prevent you from doing things that you want to do?

*"The chains of habit are too weak to be felt
until they are too strong to be broken."*

Samuel Johnson

⌒

This chapter is designed to have you become self-aware of how you have created hidden mind chains and how you can break free from them. Also, you will become more aware of how you can establish the mind chains that will accelerate your quest for high achievement.

Who Am I?

Sometimes I help, sometimes I create problems for you.

No matter how hard you try, you can't get rid of me.

Sometimes you love me. Sometimes you hate me.

If you're not aware of me, you can't change me.

I can do the most difficult tasks with ease.

I control humans and organizations.

I make you as efficient as possible.

I control you most of the time!

Who Am I?

Habits

Habits Defined

Habits are the hidden mind chains that control your daily behavior. They impact any thoughts, emotions, or behaviors you may have. They are a subconscious response to a stimulus. Habits are often thought of as a single act. However, when studied closely, they are multiple tiny acts that work in conjunction with one another, so they create a single behavior.

Consider the habits you perform when driving your car. Even as sophisticated as this may seem, driving a car entails a series of small tiny acts that are controlled in the part of your brain we discussed in the emotions chapter—your reticular activating system (RAS). As you are driving, data enters your brain through your five senses and goes to your RAS. Messages are then sent to your various body parts and you respond to successfully drive the car.

For instance, the seemingly simple process of changing lanes in heavy traffic on a 10-lane highway is, upon analysis, a series of habits. You take it for granted because you do it with such a high level of automaticity. It is really a set of habits you have developed over the years.

First, a stimulus triggers you to move a few lanes to the right. That stimulus could be that you want to exit the highway within the next mile. Next, you:

- Check your rearview and sideview mirrors to see traffic around you;

- Use the turn signal to tell other drivers of your intention to change lanes;

- Speed up or slow down to switch one lane at a time depending on the traffic around you.

- All the time you are doing these things, you are also making judgments about the spacing of the vehicles around you:

- You use your depth perception to ensure a safe lane change.

- You move the steering wheel to the right just enough to get into the next lane but not too far right to hit the car approaching in the lane to which you are moving.

- If all of a sudden, you see red taillights come on in the cars in front of you, you take your foot off the accelerator and apply pressure to the brake to slow your car. How hard you push on the brake is determined by your depth perception. If you are very close to the car in front of you, you hit the brake hard. If you're some distance from the car in front of you, you push the brake with less pressure.

- You keep repeating this process moving three lanes to the right to exit the highway.

This example has identified only a few of the multitude of complex actions and decisions made in the process of changing lanes while driving. You do most of them without thinking, at the subconscious level. They are habit patterns you have developed over years of driving.

There are hundreds of decisions you make and actions you take every day that come from your habits. Most are not a single act or thought. This is a very important point to understand. They are a combination of responses to various stimuli. Because they are hidden mind chains, you are unaware of both the actions and the level of sophistication as your brain processes multiple stimuli. This is essential information to be aware of as you go about developing new habits, which we will discuss later in the chapter.

~

"Habit is stronger than reason."
George Santayana

~

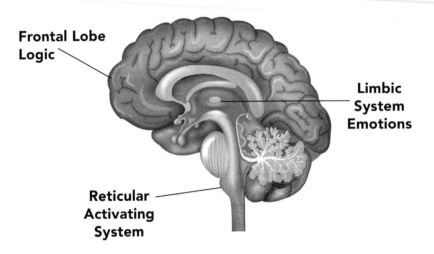

Frontal Lobe Logic

Limbic System Emotions

Reticular Activating System

Habits are formed as a result of several parts of the brain interacting with each other. The Reticular Activating System (RAS) plays a major role, just as it does for your emotions, as we examined in chapter 3. To reinforce your prior learning about the RAS, recall that it is located at the top of the brain stem. It identifies what is important and what we should ignore. Working in conjunction with other parts of your brain, the RAS has three primary functions:

1. Safety—your physical and emotional safety

2. Efficiency—create the habit patterns that cause you to function with automaticity

3. Goal Orientation—causes you to focus on those stimuli that will help you accomplish your goals

After the RAS has taken care of our safety, it works to make us perform in the most efficient manner possible. It does all it can to automate all the tasks necessary for you to function throughout each day. These tasks are related to sleeping, walking, talking, getting dressed, eating, interacting with others, problem solving, and many routine tasks such as driving. Seldom do you think about any of these functions, you just do them. That's because they have become automated by the RAS as habits.

These hidden mind chains are really neural pathways that have developed in the brain and body over time. The more an action is repeated, the deeper and more connected are the neural pathways.

Take riding a bike. If you rode a bike as a child, and then didn't ride one for years, you could probably still ride it as an adult. For example, I had not been on a bike for over 20 years. But recently, my wife and I decided to go for a bike ride. We rented bikes, got on them, and took off. Although I was a tad bit wobbly at first, my ability and comfort to ride quickly returned. Balancing on a bicycle is a difficult set of behaviors that requires sophisticated habit patterns. The neural pathways were still there, even though I had not been on a bike for decades.

The third purpose of the reticular activating system is to make us *teleological*. The word refers to having goal-oriented behavior. If you communicate to your RAS that you want to accomplish a specific goal and you tie a strong, positive, emotional component to it, the RAS will do all it can to help you accomplish the goal. To do this, the RAS sifts and sorts through thousands of stimuli per second and causes you to pay attention to only the ones that are important to the goal you want to accomplish.

"Successful people are not born that way. They become successful by establishing the habit of doing things unsuccessful people don't like to do."

William Makepeace Thackeray

Becoming Self-Aware of Your Habits

Unless you purposely focus on a habit, it will remain hidden from you. People and organizations that achieve beyond expectations are continuously monitoring their habits to ensure they result in the behaviors necessary to reach their lofty goals.

This constant self-awareness is essential because habits arise from the subconscious level. You need to monitor yourself to detect these hidden mind chains that impact your behavior in both positive and negative ways. Think about the following:

- We resort to habits whenever we are under pressure. When under pressure, some people get frustrated then angry. When under pressure, some people stay calm and in control. Do your hidden mind chains get the results you want when you are under pressure?
- Some habits allow us to perform sophisticated or complex tasks in an efficient manner. But other habits slow us down or derail our efforts to accomplish the goal. How aware are you of the hidden mind chains in complex situations?
- The effective use of habits allows you to perform an action and be metacognitive at the same time. In other words, you can act and simultaneously analyze

what you are doing. These habits have created more conscious brainpower so you can visualize other opportunities for growth and problem solving. Have you developed the hidden mind chains to do this?

How Habits Impact Your Life

Habits are repeated, automatic, subconscious emotions, thoughts, and behaviors. Research tells us that the hidden mind chains of habits control 40%–75% of daily behavior in both humans and organizations.

Habits cause automaticity, meaning you can perform a task without volition or thinking about it. The brain creates these automatic habit patterns. The brain does not differentiate between good or bad habits. It just creates them. It is both a curse and a blessing. You must decide if a habit is good or bad, helpful or hurtful.

~

"We are what we repeatedly do.
Excellence then, is not an act, but a habit."
Aristotle

~

Here are a variety of examples of where the hidden mind chains of habit patterns control your behavior:

Athletics	Exercise	Personal Interactions
Decision Making	Intimacy	Problem Solving
Dressing	Money	Recreation
Driving	Music	Self-Awareness
Eating	Non-Verbal Reactions	Sleep
Emotional Control	Parenting	Speech Patterns

Habits are learned behavior patterns, established over time. They are the brain's way of causing us to operate as efficiently as possible. Habits help you accomplish both simple and complex goals. Because of habits, much of our performance is done by rote. Because habits are hidden mind chains, it is one of the reasons they are so hard to change. They operate at a subconscious level. We must work hard to become more self-aware of our habits and how they impact our lives.

~

"Habit is either the best of servants
or the worst of masters."
Nathaniel Emmons

~

Habits are first learned by the modeling behavior of those around us when we are children. These habits are then further developed by family and societal norms as we grow into adulthood.

For example, your speech patterns are most often learned in a subconscious manner. You simply mimic what is modeled for you as an infant, then a young child. In some cases, an older person might coach you to speak in a certain manner and monitor your attempts. Your speech habits are then refined in a more conscious effort. Through continuous repetition your speech patterns become ingrained and automatic. You are unaware of these patterns until someone calls your attention to them by saying something like, "I love your southern accent."

In many endeavors, your habits are purposefully learned at the conscious level. Consider learning to play a competitive sport or being in the military. In these cases, people must perform at their best in stressful situations, without thinking. During training, military personnel and athletes work on developing precise habit patterns that will serve them best under stress. Then when they are in war or competing on the field, they can perform at an optimum level with automaticity.

Habits impact intimacy between couples. Couples develop habit patterns regarding conversation, eye contact, touching, topics, and content of conversations, empathy, love-making, and support of each other. It is not uncommon for couples to acknowledge that they are not satisfied with their intimate relationship. However, often one or both cannot explain the cause of the problem. It is just that they are unaware of the habits that negatively impact their intimate moments.

$\sim$

"Habits are at first cobwebs, then cables."

Spanish proverb

$\sim$

Habits are often a cause of job dissatisfaction. People don't like how they are treated by their boss or peers, even though those people are simply acting out of habit, unaware of how their behavior impacts others. Those people may not intentionally be acting in a rude or objectionable way; it is just their habitual patterns of speaking to others.

I have personally experienced this. In one conversation with a friend, he informed me that I frequently tell people they are wrong or that I disagree with them. My response was, "No I don't!" But in saying that, I did exactly what he said I was doing! I was totally unaware of my behavior. The weird thing is, I would not have recognized that I had disagreed until he said to me, "You just did it to me." Because he was a good friend, I was open to his feedback and didn't shut him down by trying to deny my behavior. The point of this example is that we have all kinds of habits that are hidden mind chains that impact 40%–75% of our daily behavior, which in turn affect our relationships with others.

Cuing Your Habits

Habits are automatic behavior patterns that are triggered by certain cues or stimulus. What are your habits surrounding the process of eating? These have been established by the culture in your household. The time you eat, the place you eat, what you eat, and what goes on when you are eating are all habit patterns that become ingrained and automatic. A cuing process occurs in the household that triggers actions regarding eating.

As a child, you learn how eating habits are different when you go to a friend's house for the first time and have a meal. You have certain expectations and may be startled that this family does things very differently when eating than in your house.

A more sophisticated set of habits comes into play regarding how you handle conflict situations. If you have grown up in a family culture that has people shouting and getting angry anytime a disagreement erupts, you most likely have developed the same habit.

Because of your family culture, you have learned that you must aggressively defend yourself when told you are wrong and work to *win* the argument. When you are told you are wrong, it cues the hostile behaviors you have observed as you were growing up: defensiveness, shouting, name calling, finger pointing, closed mindedness. You then mimic those behaviors.

On the other hand, as you were growing up, if you experienced people acknowledging frustrations in a calm manner who then began to work collaboratively at problem solving, that is most likely what you do. When there was a difference of opinion, people discussed with an open mind and without defensiveness. There is a sharing and vigorous, but respectful, discussion of opinions. You may even agree to disagree. This was a very different set of habits than observed in the first scenario.

⁓

"Our character is basically a composite of our habits. Because they are consistent, often unconscious patterns, they constantly, daily, express our character."
Stephen Covey

⁓

Organizational Habits

Long-term, high achievement in athletics, music, art, math, science, business, industry, or in your family all have one common characteristic. People *habitually* do all the things necessary to maintain the high level of performance.

The development of these high-performance habits is a conscious effort. In these situations, people in leadership positions initiate and support the implementation of the high-achievement habits.

Organizations have habits as well. In organizations, the habit patterns (i.e., the repeated, automatic, subconscious collective thoughts, behaviors, and emotions) are called *culture* or *traditions*.

High-performing organizations have leaders who explicitly develop a culture and traditions that support continuous high achievement. These organizations are full of high-performing people with similar habits. This happens because the leaders purposely work to create the desired habits. Then they continuously monitor to ensure that these habits are supportive of the high-achievement goals. Leaders in high-achieving companies understand how employee performance is controlled by the culture/traditions.

In high-achieving organizations, once the leader has established the culture, team members take responsibility for reinforcing the culture. This reinforcement is accomplished through peer pressure. Group members take pride in and reward each other's successes. When something doesn't go well, they immediately begin to analyze the problem and determine corrective behaviors. The hidden mind chains of habits control much of their behavior in a positive way.

~

"Winners make a habit of doing
things losers don't want to do."

Lucas Remmerswaal

~

Conversely, in underperforming organizations, no one takes responsibility to determine what habits might be derailing or stalling progress toward goals. No one is aware that their poor performance is controlled by unproductive habits. This lack of self-awareness regarding the organizational culture is why there is underachievement year after year. The hidden negative mind chains of habits control much of their behavior.

A Comparison of Habitual Behavior Patterns

In my years as a leadership and performance coach, I have observed how the culture and traditions impact individual and company performance during turbulent times. Here's an example of a sophisticated, habitual decision-making process. Many people habitually follow this process when they're making decisions in their personal or business life:

1. Become aware that there is a problem

2. Determine the real cause of the problem

3. Brainstorm multiple potential solutions to solve the problem

4. Analyze the impact of each of the potential solutions

5. Determine the people and resources needed to implement the most effective solution

6. Provide resources and training needed to implement the solution

7. Determine criteria to evaluate the effectiveness of the solution when implemented

8. Implement the solution

9. Monitor to ensure they are getting the desired results

10. Reinforce or change behavior depending on the results

This is a sophisticated, complex process that has been implemented so frequently that people do it with automaticity. It is a positive hidden mind chain. It's the way they do things in their personal or corporate life to achieve beyond expectations.

*"Good habits are the key to all success.
Bad habits are the unlocked door to failure."*

Og Mandino

~

Here's a contrasting example I have observed of how some people or groups make decisions in their personal or business life:

1. Become aware that there is a problem

2. Focus on the symptoms of the problem rather than the cause of the problem

3. Identify a potential solution for the problem

4. Implement the solution

5. Attempt to deal with frustrations that arise because people don't have the knowledge or skill to implement the solution

6. Attempt to deal with other problems that arise because the original problem was not resolved

7. Move on to another problem even though the original problem has not been resolved

This process does not yield the same positive results of the first example you read. Because of these habit patterns, the person or group becomes frustrated and stressed, often to the point of thinking they are overwhelmed. They experience a constant, never-ending barrage of problems that never get solved.

Both the first and second examples of decision-making habit patterns are very real. I have consulted with organizations and people who have used both. People and organizations develop patterns of doing things. These patterns become automatic no matter how sophisticated the process being implemented. The most important question is, how aware are you of habit patterns that impact every aspect of your life?

~

"If you are going to achieve excellence in big things,
you develop the habit in little matters.
Excellence is not an exception; it is a prevailing attitude."
Colin Powell

~

Changing and Creating New Habits

All of us have attempted to change habits. We all have struggled with this process. We've had varying degrees of success. Many of us feel we have not been as successful as we want.

When you are consciously developing a new habit, you must determine if the new habit is a competing or non-competing habit. A competing habit is created to refine or replace an existing habit. With competing habits, there is going to be a battle between the old and new habits. The old habit does not want the new one infringing on its territory so it will fight the new habit. An example of a competing habit is any habit you have related to eating. If you are going to change a habit related to what you eat, how much you eat, and when you eat, there will be a competition between the new and old habits.

The old habits play dirty. They establish their own rules for the contest. They will use your own emotions to keep you from developing the new habit. The old habits will make you feel like you are depriving yourself of something you really enjoy. The old habits will be sending you messages through your self-talk that it is "much simpler and more comfortable just to keep the old habit!"

When there are new habits competing with old habits, it's harder and uncomfortable trying to embed the new habit. To embed the new competing habit, you must be aware of and deal with each of the following:

- You must purposely develop knowledge and skills for the new habit. This takes time and has its own frustrations.

- You must work to stop the old habit and simultaneously start the new one to replace the old one. This creates a powerful, emotional tug-of-war. The old one does not want to be changed and will fight you.

- You are going to experience frustration or worse as you work to stop the old habit. These negative emotions are generated by the slow progress and spotty success you have trying to establish the new habit.

- You must combat people who, knowingly or unknowingly, put roadblocks in your way as you work to stop the old habit and develop the new habit.

- You must continue all other activities in your life. Any of these can distract your efforts for stopping the old habit and developing the new habit.

You can establish a new competing habit. To do it, you must be aware of the obstacles listed above and prepare to overcome them.

~

"People do not decide their futures, they decide their habits and their habits decide their futures."

F. M. Alexander

~

When developing new habits, you are developing new neural pathways in your nervous system. Neural pathways are like a hiking trail. The more you walk on the trail, the more pronounced it becomes. The same thing happens with habits and neural pathways. The longer you have used that pathway, the harder it is to change. For example, if a 16-year-old and a 40-year-old want to change eating habits, the 16-year-old is likely to have an easier time because the neural pathways are not as pronounced as is the 40-year-old. The more you have used the neural pathway, the more difficult it is to change. You are on autopilot. You don't think about the eating habit, you just do it at a subconscious level.

This is why a non-competing habit is actually easier to develop than a competing one. A non-competing habit can be developed without causing direct interference with an existing one. For example, if you are going to learn a new hobby for which you have had no previous experience (e.g., knitting, photography, tennis, or chess), embedding a non-competing habit is easier because there are no existing habits to rear their ugly heads and try to hinder your effort.

Of course, you still will have to deal with emotions related to how much effort and time it takes to embed a new habit. You must develop the neural pathways and then the muscle memory to embed a new habit. But you can focus all of your attention on the development of this new habit instead of having to also fight an old habit.

Any time you are working on a new habit, there will be ups and downs. In chapter 5, "Expectations Determine Your Reality," you will read about the four developmental stages you go through whenever you want to develop a new skill. Please understand that it's normal for you to go through these ups and downs when developing any new habit.

Nine-Step Process to Replace a Habit

The hardest work in changing habits is when you are seeking to replace an old habit with a new competing one. This requires establishing a new mindset. But here's where the really hard work begins. The old habit is going to fight like mad to keep its power. For the old habit, this is a fight to the death! During this battle, you must deal with various emotions that rise up as old habits fight the change. Overcoming these negative emotions is your most important task as you establish your new habit pattern.

As part of your mindset, you have to accept that it will take time and be a long-term process requiring hundreds of repetitions. You may have read or heard that you can change a habit in as little as three weeks. Most valid research studies question the accuracy of this statement. Forming a new habit more likely requires hundreds and hundreds of correct, successful repetitions. You need all the following to make a competing new habit replace an established old one:

- the knowledge and skills you need related to the new habit
- the environment in which you find yourself when implementing it
- the focus and intensity you place on the process

- the support or coaching you receive as you go through the repetitions to create the neural pathways necessary to form the habit

Here is the Nine-Step Process to Replace Habit. First the process is described. It is followed by a very specific example of how the process was used to create a new, sophisticated habit pattern.

Write in your journal your new habit goal. For this goal, identify and *write down* multiple positive emotions and effects that will occur as a result of creating this new habit pattern. As you work through the process, *continually remind yourself of these positives*, especially when you're experiencing some challenges with implementation.

Once you have your goal and positive emotions and effects, write down your responses to the items below.

1. Become aware of existing habits that will support your new habit pattern goal. Determine how you can use them to support the development of your new habit patterns.

2. Become aware of habits that will hinder the accomplishment of your new habit pattern. Determine how you will counter these habits.

3. Become aware of emotions that will hinder development of the new habit pattern. Determine how you will counter these emotions.

4. Become aware of what triggers the old habit that must be changed. Determine how to respond each time you recognize the trigger. *This is a critical point in the development of the new habit.*

5. Formally or informally enlist the services of a coach, mentor, or friend to provide emotional and intellectual support. These people are integral to your success.

6. Become aware of knowledge and skills needed to implement the new habit patterns.

   a. Determine how and when you will acquire this new knowledge/skill.

   b. Develop the knowledge and skills necessary to avoid the inevitable emotion commotion that will arise as you work at embedding the new habit patterns.

7. Become aware of others who have developed the habit patterns you want to develop. Determine where you can observe these people modeling the habit patterns that you want to create. These people may become part of your support network.

8. Visualize yourself implementing the desired habit patterns based on the models you observe.

9. Use self-talk to remind yourself of the desired habit patterns and to reinforce yourself when you have implemented the desired behavior.

∼

"If your habits don't line up with your dream,
then you need to either change your habits or change
your dream."
John Maxwell

∼

Let's look at an example of this process that I personally used to be more effective working with people.

Habit goal: Develop the habit patterns necessary to empathize with people.

Positive emotions and effects: To be more effective working with people, I must develop the habit of being empathetic. By establishing this new habit, I will enjoy more positive interactions and reduce emotion commotion.

1. Become aware of existing habits that will support your new habit pattern goal. Determine how you will use them to support the development of your new habit patterns.

    a. *Habits that will support empathizing goal:* good listener, notetaker, task oriented

    b. *How they will support development of my empathizing goal:* make empathizing the "task" I must do. Use listening and note-taking habits to identify info that can be used to empathize.

2. Become aware of habits that hinder accomplishment of the new habit patterns. Determine how you will counter these habits.

    a. *Habits that hinder accomplishment of empathizing goal:* task orientation habit; habit of making tasks more important than people

    b. *How these habit patterns will be countered:* make my "task" empathizing; make the task "taking time with and listening to people and taking notes."

3. Become aware of emotions that will hinder development of the new habit patterns. Determine how you will counter these emotions.

    a. *Emotions that hinder development of habit patterns to be developed:* my impatience, frustration, irritation when I feel someone is distracting my efforts to accomplish the task

   b. *How the emotions will be countered:* recognize and take pride in slowing down to pay attention to people's reactions and feeling state. This information is providing the raw data to accomplish the "task" of empathizing.

4. Become aware of what triggers the old habit patterns. Determine how to respond each time you recognize the trigger.

   a. *Identify what triggers the habit patterns to be changed:* my feelings of impatience, frustration, irritation because "task" is not getting done. Make the task "taking time with and listening to people and taking notes.

   b. *Response to the trigger:* my negative feelings and negative self-talk about people is my trigger. I must replace these with: "STOP, PAUSE, LISTEN" to what someone is saying. With this information I should trigger my new habit patterns for empathizing skills.

5. Formally or informally enlist the services of a coach, mentor, or friend to provide emotional and intellectual support. These people are integral to your success.

   a. *People who can help:* Paula, Sherry, Beth, Debbie

6. Become aware of knowledge and skills needed to implement the new habit patterns.

   a. *Develop knowledge and skills needed:* attend Effective Communication and Skillful Listening workshop. Also talk with Paula, Sherry, Beth, and Debbie about empathizing skills.

    b. *Develop emotional control skills:* focus on stopping the negative judgments about people who are "slowing down task accomplishment" by expressing concerns. Realize they are not trying to sabotage the task. They have legitimate concerns that must be heard and analyzed. "Listening" to them must become my primary task.

7. Become aware of others who have developed the habit patterns you want to develop. Determine where you can observe these people modeling the habit patterns you want to create. These people may become part of your support network.

    a. *People to observe:* Paula, Sherry, Beth, Debbie

    b. *Observe each:* any time I'm in their presence to see how they show empathy, watch them model what they told me to do and what I learned in the workshops.

8. Visualize yourself implementing the desired habit patterns based on the models.

    a. Pull up the "video in my head" of the modeling examples from the four mentors and compare that to what I did in discussions with people. Work to mimic the examples of the four mentors.

    b. Ask the four mentors to give me feedback any time they are a part of a work group I am in.

9. Use self-talk to remind yourself of the desired habit patterns and to reinforce when you have implemented the desired habit patterns.

   a. *Self-talk I will use:* when a trigger occurs say, "Slow down, pay attention to concerns; your task—empathize."

   b. *Analyze, using self-talk:* ask myself, "What would Debbie say here? How have you seen Sherry handle this?" Use self-talk to compare my performance to the models I have in my head from the four mentors.

   c. *Compliment myself:* each time I recognize a trigger and start implementing empathizing skills; when I analyze in comparison to the four mentors model, compliment myself on what I did correctly.

~

"Habits are where are our lives and
careers and bodies are made."

Seth Godin

~

Many of you may be thinking, "Gosh, this is so complicated. It's too much! You have to set a goal and follow a long nine-step plan. How can I do that?"

Here's a thought to consider. We know from the research that every habit is established following this same process! In fact, there are scores of highly-promoted weight-loss programs. The ones that have the most success use a process very similar to what you have just read in this nine-step process.

Most importantly, if you have successfully changed a habit in the past, you unknowingly used a version of this nine-step process. You were just not aware it was happening! In fact, you have probably used this nine-step process to develop all of your existing habits regarding things such as:

- interacting with significant others
- learning to drive a car
- preparing a meal
- your morning routine getting ready for work
- socializing with friends
- studying in school
- doing big projects at work
- playing a musical instrument
- developing an athletic skill

Musicians, artists, actors, and athletes use these steps on a continual basis. You don't play a concerto without developing specific habits that enable you to play with automaticity. Anyone achieving beyond expectations has developed habit patterns that allow them to operate with automaticity.

By using the nine-step process, you'll be communicating to your reticular activating system what is important to you. You're telling the RAS to screen out those stimuli that are not going to be helpful to you and to cause you to focus on those stimuli that will be helpful.

Be aware that the reticular activating system will slip back to those old habits unless you are consciously reminding it to pay attention to the new one. This is where self-talk becomes so important. By using the self-talk, you are consciously reminding your RAS that this is the new direction you want to go.

Over time, the new neural pathways will be developed, and it will become a habit. Continually remind yourself that developing a new habit takes many repetitions. You will experience success and setbacks, and the progress will be slow, *but* it is worth it.

Your Self-Talk and Changing Habits

Step nine of the process is about your self-talk. Let's look more closely at this. If your self-talk is negative it will hinder achievement. If your self-talk is positive or instructive, it will guide and support achievement.

There are three categories of self-talk:

- *Cues/instruction for a specific activity*—words that remind you of key points in an activity. For example, when I was developing my empathizing habits, key words I used were *stop, pause, listen.* I used these to cause me to identify the feelings or message the person was sending. A powerful tool to develop new habits is to use self-talk to cue your behavior or thinking.

- *Positive emotional support*—words you say to yourself to stay positive and focused no matter what is happening. Examples are: *it's tough, but you can do it; stay focused; you'll figure it out; patience; way to go.* It's important to use encouraging words to maintain a positive and productive mindset. When you hear something often enough, you believe it. It is a form of personal mind control that triggers your brain to release the hormones that will be helpful to you in that situation.

- *Intrinsic rewards*—this is where you tell yourself you did a good job. Recognizing the smallest success through self-talk is critical to changing a habit. It helps maintain the positive mindset to overcome the mishaps you will encounter changing a habit. The purpose is to develop pride and self-efficacy. Tell yourself what you have done well. Examples: *yes, you did it!; way to summarize the feelings he just expressed; my patience paid off, good job.*

~

"Watch your thoughts: they become words.
Watch your words: they become actions.
Watch your actions: they become habits.
Watch your habits: they become character.
Watch your character: it becomes your destiny."

Frank Outlaw

~

Changing Intellectual and Emotional Habits

Changing habits in relation to intellectual skills uses the same nine-step process. Think back to when you were learning how to add, subtract, multiply, and divide. It was a ponderous process to begin, but after hundreds of repetitions you developed automaticity with these mathematical processes. The same process applies to writing sentences and paragraphs. These are sophisticated intellectual processes that you have automated to enable you to function in a more efficient manner.

Changing and learning habits related to your emotional skills is the most complex. When you experience an emotional situation, positive or negative, you operate out of habit. Not only are the hidden mind chains in full force, you must also deal with the powerful hormones raging through your body trying to get you to fight or flee. Emotions significantly cloud logical thinking. So, your frontal lobe must operate at full force to offset the raging hormones triggering the emotion commotion.

~

"First, we form habits, then they form us.
Conquer your bad habits or they will conquer you."
Rob Gilbert

~

Emotional Habit Activity

Here is an activity for you to become more self-aware of your emotional habits. There are seven examples of behavior people exhibit when they feel an emotional threat. As you read each one, record in your journal the number of the behaviors that you have experienced when you have felt challenged, disrespected, overwhelmed, embarrassed, or any other negative emotion:

1. Withdraw physically from the situation.
2. Exhibit physical behaviors such as looking down, shaking, clutching your chest, wringing your hands, or tearing up.
3. Make a verbal defense.
4. Blame someone else, take no responsibility.
5. Become verbally aggressive.

6. Become physically aggressive.

7. Monitor your feelings and wonder what is causing them to happen.

In your journal, please write your answers to the following.

A. How many numbers did you write down?

B. For each number you wrote down, think about the behavior. How often do use this behavior: seldom, sometimes, often? Write one of these three words by each behavior.

C. Now summarize your information. Write your thoughts from this brief analysis of your emotional habits.

You must be aware of a habit before you can change it. Write in your journal the answer to this question: Because of this activity, what emotional habits do you want to change?

In the list of emotional reactions, note item seven, "Monitor your feelings and wonder what is causing them to happen." The other six examples demonstrate that the person is beginning to experience emotion commotion. Item seven is different than the others. It is an example of a hidden mind chain that was developed to enable the person to maintain emotional control. As you learned in chapter 3, by using your frontal lobe, you have the ability to monitor and decide how you are going to respond in any situation. To achieve beyond expectations, it is important to establish number seven as a habit pattern.

If you are going to change emotional habits, pay attention any time you experience the thoughts and behaviors listed in items one to six. These responses are automatic behaviors; they are hidden mind chains that most people are unaware of when they exhibit them. These behaviors must trigger your new thinking and new emotional habit patterns you want to develop.

Foundational Habits to Make the Impossible, Possible

Throughout this chapter you have read about the impact of habits on all aspects of your behavior. You have become more aware of how your brain works to create habits. Also, you have read about what needs to be done if you want to change a habit. This final section is going to identify and discuss the most foundational habits to make the impossible, possible.

As you are aware, all the habits that will help you achieve beyond expectations are of a positive nature. They all cause you to function in a productive manner, especially in challenging situations. You need these hidden mind chains working for you if you want to make the impossible, possible. These habits will inspire your very best performance.

Here are the foundational habits to make the impossible, possible! You must develop and finely hone these habits:

1. **Passion** as a habit

2. **Positivity** as a habit

3. **Time Management** as a habit

4. **Resilience** as a habit

5. **Action Orientation** as a habit

6. **Intuition** as a habit

7. **Persistence** as a habit

As you are reading about each of these foundational habits, compare what you are reading to your daily habitual behavior. Which of the foundational habits are you using on a consistent basis? Which do you need to use more often?

1. Passion as a Habit

Passion is an intense, difficult-to-control emotion that rockets you to your goal. Here's how:

- Passion demonstrates the conviction you have to accomplish your goal.
- Passion communicates the importance of your goal.
- Passion is where you go all out with such intensity that others may view you as unbalanced!
- Passion means you intentionally step outside your comfort zone to accomplish your goal.
- Passion powers an intensity of focus that cannot be denied. Your intense feelings energize you to overcome any obstacles to accomplish your goal.
- Passion means you're totally invested to do whatever it takes to achieve your goal. No great deed was ever accomplished without passion.
- Passion is compelling.
- Passion sparks unlimited enthusiasm and energy.
- Passion compels your ambition to succeed no matter the circumstances.
- Passion motivates you.
- Passion is contagious; it motivates others.

When you are passionate and surround yourself with passionate people, you will achieve beyond expectations.

Some may criticize you for your passion. Some may say you are out of control or crazy. These people are often the ones unwilling to take risks. What you are attempting to do may frighten others because they are unwilling to step outside their comfort zone. They may be people who enjoy staying with the status quo. Whatever drives them to criticize you comes from their personal beliefs and values. They are comfortable with their beliefs and values and that is great for them.

You, on the other hand, have your own set of values and beliefs that drive your passion. If you want to take on their values and beliefs, then listen to and follow their advice. If you want to be driven by your values and beliefs, stoke your passion to a raging inferno. Go for it. It is your life. You need to do what is best for you if your goal is to make the impossible, possible.

$\sim$

"Achieving beyond expectations requires you
to overcome obstacles beyond expectations.
Passion is the fuel that powers your quest."
Bill Blokker, EdD

$\sim$

2. Positivity as a Habit

Positivity is the cornerstone for all achievement. It is the stabilizing force needed to have your brain and body work to its optimum ability.

- Positivity is focusing on possibilities rather than limitations.
- Positivity is being confident, constructive, encouraging, and upbeat.

- Positivity is focusing on what can be learned when disaster strikes.
- Positivity is turning toxic situations into constructive situations.
- Positivity is when you look for the good in life.
- Positivity is appreciating what you have and expressing gratitude to others.
- Positivity is learning from the past and focusing on possibilities in the present or future.
- Positivity is making the best of bad situations.
- Positivity is initiating actions rather than waiting for them to happen.
- Positivity is a conscious choice to be optimistic and use constructive self-talk when faced with challenges and difficult times.
- Positivity is inspiring others to perform at their best.
- Positivity maintains a healthy chemical balance in your body.

There are those who will be critical of your positivity. They will say you have a "Pollyanna" attitude. You may be called a phony because, "No one can always be as happy, upbeat and positive as you. It's unreal. You're putting it on." People will criticize you for not being "tough enough," because you don't point out mistakes of others. People will say you're not strong because you don't yell at people to get them motivated. The people who take these positions are either unaware of or don't know how to implement the research on the brain. They don't understand that the brain functions at its best in positive and supportive situations. The brain will allow you to take the greatest risks when there is a supportive structure available to assist when needed. Also, these people have not internalized how negative thinking creates toxins in your body that paralyzes your performance.

~

"Once you replace negative thoughts with positive ones, you'll start having positive results."
Willie Nelson

~

3. Time Management as a Habit

Time management means controlling your use of time to most efficiently accomplish the task/goal. The habit of time management results from multiple brain routines working in conjunction with each other.

- Time management starts with self-awareness regarding your time usage.
- Time management is self-discipline regarding goal focus.
- Time management is delegating to others.
- Time management is using data to drive behavior.
- Time management is monitoring activity and adjusting behavior to get desired results.
- Time management is establishing and sticking to productive routines.
- Time management minimizes down time by having a "to-do" checklist.
- Time management is establishing and adhering to priorities.

In chapter 2, you read about the Eisenhower Priority Process. As you recall, this is a process to establish your priorities. The habit of time management is all about having a clear set of priorities that drives all of your behavior. If you have not already started using the Eisenhower Priority Process to establish priorities in your life, try applying it now to improve your habits. It will pave the way for you to achieve beyond expectations.

Be aware, time thieves are everywhere! Time thieves may be coworkers, your boss, family, or friends. Intentionally or unintentionally, they will interrupt and distract you from your task. You must take steps to eliminate or minimize these interruptions and distractions.

However, the most dangerous time thieves are the subtle ones inside your own head! Here is a list of time thieves lurking in the shadows of your mind waiting to steal your time:

- procrastination
- disorganization
- refusing to delegate
- socializing
- unwilling to say "no"
- multi-tasking

These are habits that you unintentionally developed. You personally trigger or facilitate each of these time thieves. Increase your self-awareness about these time thieves. You must determine what are you doing to steal your own time. Once you have this self-awareness, you must monitor and adjust your thinking, habit, and behavior.

It is most critical that you develop effective time-management habits. *Time is your most valuable and limited resource.* Once you have lost time, you never get it back. To achieve beyond expectations, you must protect and efficiently use every second you are given. Develop strong time-management habits.

~

"Life is 10% what happens to us and
90% how we react to it."

Dennis P. Kimbro

~

4. Resilience as a Habit

Resilience is the intellectual and emotional capacity to dismiss misfortune and move ahead with enthusiasm and determination.

- Resilience is your ability to overcome negative thoughts or feelings regarding a lack of success.

- Resilience means you bounce back from adversity.

- Resilience is your ability to regain your form and shape.

- Resilient people are driven by the passion for their goal.

- Resilient people are optimistic.

- Resilient people have a high level of self-efficacy.

- Resilient people embrace change.

- Resilient people are creative problem solvers.

- Resilient people are action oriented.

- Resilient people improve each day.

- Resilient people rise from the ashes.

- Resilient people refuse to let anguish destroy their optimism about their future.

Resilience is learned. Children learn it from modeling behavior of significant others in their lives. The habit of resilience is a result of your mindset when experiencing a setback. Resilience results when you do the following:

- Expect setbacks to occur. They are unavoidable no matter how hard you try to eliminate them. Use your frontal lobe to override the potential negative feelings you may have about the setback.

- When you experience a setback, look at it as a learning experience.

  o You have just learned something that has not worked.

  o Believe you have the knowledge and skill to identify a solution to the problem.

- Kick your brain into the creative and flexible zone. Think outside the box. You have the wherewithal to identify a solution.

- Act. Nothing happens until something happens. You may not have the best solution but acting on what you got will determine how close you are to success. Avoid analysis paralysis.

- Use positive, optimistic self-talk. It is essential to trigger constructive action in order to succeed.

~

"A problem is your chance to do your best."
Duke Ellington

~

5. Action Oriented as a Habit

When you are action orientated, you respond to tasks or challenges in a prompt and definitive manner. Nothing happens until something happens. When you are action oriented, things happen.

- Action oriented means you have a clear sense of purpose.
- Action oriented means you avoid analysis paralysis.
- Action oriented means you establish and stick to a timeline of tasks.
- Action oriented means you control and defeat ambiguity.
- Action oriented means you inspire a sense of urgency in self and others.
- Action oriented means you demonstrate self-efficacy.
- Action oriented means you initiate projects with small, easily accomplished steps.
- Action oriented means you have a mindset of, "if it is to be, it is up to me."
- Action oriented means you solve the problem rather than trying to place blame.
- Action oriented means you pioneer solutions to get the job done.

When you are action oriented, you will find people who put roadblocks in your way. These people will claim you are moving too fast. They will say you don't have enough information. They will emphasize *risks*. These people will point out the ways you can fail.

There are many reasons why people put up roadblocks. No matter the amount of time and brain power put into analyzing data, some people will feel uncomfortable moving forward. Making the impossible, possible requires action. The bottom line—nothing happens until something happens. Make something happen! You will never have all the information needed to make a decision or start a project. Trust your gut. Achieving beyond expectation requires action-oriented habits.

6. Intuition as a Habit

Intuition is a thought you have about something, but you don't know why. You don't have any conscious, concrete evidence to support your thinking. It just feels right! Intuition results from your subconscious brain synthesizing past experiences and current events. Your subconscious brain sifts and sorts all of your prior experiences. It recognizes patterns. Then it looks at those patterns, combines new information and makes predictions of what is best moving forward. The result: suddenly you have an *aha!*, although you don't know where it came from. Intuition is a message being sent by your subconscious to your conscious brain.

∿

"Intuition is more powerful than intellect."
Steve Jobs

∿

Intuition occurs when you are talking to someone. You are hearing the words he is saying, but you are not believing him. Your intuition is telling you that you can't trust what he is saying. Here's what is happening in your subconscious brain. You're getting stimulus from your five senses. Your subconscious is noticing body language—the non-verbal communication being sent to you—and your hearing is detecting tone, volume, and speed of speaking. Your eyes are taking in information and processing it. This information is combined with prior knowledge. As a result, your subconscious sends the message not to trust what is being said.

~

"I've trusted the still, small voice of intuition
my entire life. And the only time I've made
mistakes is when I didn't listen."
Oprah Winfrey

~

You must trust your intuition. Your intuition wants what you value most and tries to find a way to make that happen. To do this, your subconscious mind pays attention to the goal you want to achieve, the patterns it has formed from previous experiences, and the incoming data from your senses. The synthesis of this data leads the subconscious to form conclusions that are communicated to the conscious brain. Develop the habit of intuitive thinking. It will help you achieve beyond expectations.

7. Persistence as a Habit

Persistence is your continuous drive to accomplish a goal no matter what obstacles are put in your way.

- Persistence means you work until the goal is accomplished.
- Persistence means you learn from unsuccessful attempts and move forward with modified solutions.

- Persistence is putting the elation of accomplishing your goal above the pain you endure to overcome the obstacles.

- Persistence means that you use emotional control to avoid emotion commotion.

- Persistence means you develop creative solutions to overcome obstacles.

- Persistence means you are dedicated.

- Persistence means you have endurance.

- Persistence means you have grit and determination.

- Persistence means you are insistent.

- Persistence means you are tireless in your effort to achieve beyond expectations.

No matter what you're trying to achieve, you will experience detours and roadblocks. Some will be minor, others gigantic. When you have the habit of persistence, you will encounter these roadblocks and automatically begin to think about the strategies necessary to overcome them. We must realize that frustration, anger, and disappointment are all a waste of time and energy. These negative emotions do nothing to assist in eliminating the roadblock. In fact, they actually prevent your mind from coming up with creative solutions! The habit of persistence triggers your immediate focus on alternative solutions so you can accomplish your goal.

How to Implement the Foundational Habits
to Make the Impossible, Possible

You are reading this book because you want to get better at what you do. No matter your goal, you need the foundational habits if you intend to succeed. You must train your brain to develop these habits to achieve beyond expectations.

Here is a brain training activity. Follow this process to establish these foundational habits in your brain so you can make the impossible, possible! Write your responses to each of these items in your journal:

1. Go back and analyze each of the foundational habits.

2. For each habit, determine on a scale of 1–10 (low to high) how much this habit plays a role in your life, at present.

3. For any habit with a score of seven or lower, determine how you will strengthen or raise that habit to a score of at least eight.

4. Next establish your priorities. Which of the habits do you need to strengthen? Which one is the most important, second most important, third most important? Write them down in priority order.

5. Now create a plan for the development of the habit you identified as the most important to strengthen. Refer to the Nine-Step Process to Replace a Habit to develop your written plan.

6. Implement your plan. Make sure you monitor and adjust your efforts. Most importantly, celebrate your smallest successes.

7. After you feel you have upgraded your habit to an eight or higher, move on to the next one you identified as second most important and work on that. Repeat the process for each other habit.

What Are Your Next Steps?

As you read in the first chapter, knowledge is power only when it is applied to daily living. So, what are you going to apply from this chapter to your daily living?

Habits can be a positive or negative force in your life. It's your choice. It is essential that you become aware of your habit patterns to determine what's controlling your life.

New habit patterns can be developed. Just remember that the development of new habits is challenging, time consuming and an arduous task. As you work to develop the new habit patterns, make extensive use of self-talk to guide your efforts. Be realistic. You will have setbacks. Expect them. Most important, focus on your successful efforts. Then move forward with more determination than ever.

All people who achieve beyond expectations have developed the habits to make it happen. Anyone who has made the impossible, possible has worked diligently to create the neural pathways to function in the most efficient and effective manner possible. You have the knowledge of what needs to be done. What are you going to do with it?

~

"My dreams are worthless, my plans are dust,
my goals are impossible.
All are of no value unless they are
followed by action."

Og Mandino

~

Use the questions on the next page and the content of this chapter to guide your planning. Write your responses in your journal.

1. What was something you read and thought was really important?
2. What are you going to apply immediately?
3. How are you going to take steps to become more self-aware of the hidden mind chains that control up to 75% of your daily behavior?
    a. Are those mind chains helping or hindering your dreams?
    b. Are you their slave or are they your servant?

Key Points: Habits—Your Hidden Mind Chains

1. Habits control 40%–75% of your daily activities, emotions, thinking, and body functions.

2. Habits are the subconscious patterns, neural pathways, your brain creates to have you operate as efficiently as possible.

3. People have habits. Organizations have culture and traditions that function just as habits do for people. Culture/traditions are far more powerful in controlling employee behavior than the organization's formal policies/procedures.

4. Habits can be either productive or harmful. It is essential that you become aware of how habits impact your behavior to ensure they are supporting your goal achievement.

5. You must be aware of a habit before you can change it. The Nine-Step Process to Replace a Habit outlines how to create new habits. Changing a habit is a time-consuming process and takes many months of consistent effort.

6. Self-talk is an essential tool for changing habits. There are three types of self-talk:

   a. Cues/instruction

   b. Positive emotional support

   c. Intrinsic rewards

7. The foundational habits necessary to achieve beyond expectations:

   a. Passion

   b. Positivity

   c. Time Management

   d. Resilience

   e. Action Oriented

   f. Intuition

   g. Persistence

~

"A hidden mind chain is saying, 'I can't.
Replace that habit with, 'I can."
Bill Blokker, EdD

~

5

Expectations Determine Your Reality

Shannon was an excellent soccer player in high school. She also played on a premier-level traveling team. Shannon had expectations of playing collegiate soccer, but was told by the coach of her premier team that she wasn't good enough to play at any four-year college. He said she might be able to play at the community college level. No college recruited her to play soccer.

Shannon's family was not able to provide financial help to pay for college. If she was going to go, she would need to pay the whole bill herself. People continually discouraged her from going to college. Their advice: get a job! The people around Shannon had low expectations of her. But she was determined she was going to find a way to accomplish her goal of a college degree and playing collegiate soccer.

Sue, the mother of one of Shannon's high school friends, heard about Shannon's situation. Sue had two sons who were college soccer players and she knew all about applying for financial aid. Shannon and Sue worked diligently to overcome the obstacles. Shannon applied and was admitted to a university with a good women's soccer team. She convinced the women's soccer coach to let her try out for the team. Shannon made the team but the coach told her she was unlikely to play much in her first year. Shannon maintained her high expectations. She worked persistently on all the skills and conditioning to excel at soccer. By her sophomore year, she was a starter on the college soccer team.

Shannon graduated in four years. The next year she earned her MBA. She was hired, immediately, in a high-paying job. Shannon is now the Senior Director for Corporate Partnerships for a California university.

Expectations determine your reality. You just need to decide which expectations you will allow to determine your reality. Shannon had to make a conscious decision about which expectations she would allow to determine her reality. Many people had low expectations for her. Many discouraged her. She couldn't afford college. She had to overcome huge obstacles. Shannon chose to have her high expectations determine her reality. It was a constant battle pushing away all naysayers. Shannon achieved beyond expectations because of her belief in herself, her persistence, creative problem solving, and a little support from a friend.

Holding high expectations for yourself is the only way for you to achieve your full potential. Having high expectations may frighten you. That's okay. Nothing of value is achieved in this world without causing you to stretch and feel discomfort.

This chapter will provide you with an abundance of information about expectations:

- the hidden nature of expectations
- how expectations impact your behavior
- how to combat low expectations
- how to deal with unrealistic expectations
- specific strategies to achieve your high expectations.

~

"High achievement always takes place in the framework of high expectations."

Charles F. Kettering

~

The Hidden Nature of Expectations

Expectations are sneaky and complex. Most often people are unaware expectations are influencing them. If *your* expectations are going to determine *your* reality, you must become aware of the insidious nature of expectations coming from others and our culture. You must increase your awareness of when and how expectations are influencing you.

Expectations are beliefs, opinions, views, or ideas that people hold about themselves or others. Part of the hidden nature of expectations is that there are many words people use to communicate expectations. Here's how some sound in conversations:

- "I *anticipate* the meeting is going to go smoothly."
- "My *suspicion* is he will be very angry."
- "My *view* is that it doesn't matter what we do. It won't make a difference."
- "My *intention* was to get her to understand the intricacies of this job."
- "I *assume* Carlos and Jennifer will support us and I *hope* Shaun and Scott will too."
- "My *goal* is to complete this by January."
- "My *calculation* is that it will take twice as long."

All the italicized words communicate the idea of expectations. An expectation is any time a person makes a statement or has an opinion about something. Whether they use the word expectation or any of the others, they are still identifying beliefs, opinions, views, or ideas. Here's a list of many words that express expectations.

Expectation-Related Words

Anticipate	Goal	Projection
Assume	Hope	Suspicion
Belief	Inference	Supposition
Calculation	Intention	Surmise
Desire	Opinion	Thesis
Feeling	Prediction	Theory
Forecast	Premise	View

There are three categories of expectations:

- Expectations we have of ourselves
- Expectations we have of others
- Expectations others have of us

Expectations originate from your parents, family, significant others, friends, schoolmates, as well as your religious traditions, culture, and nowadays from social media. They control your reality from birth and continue until you die.

For example, parents and family consciously and unconsciously set expectations about how males and females are supposed to act as soon as the child is born. The expectations for female/male behavior may differ depending on your race, ethnicity, or geographical area of the country, but they are always powerful. Depending on the sex of the child, expectations may determine:

- the kind of baby gifts given;
- the words used to describe the newborn child;
- the advice others give the new parents;
- "acceptable" ways for the child to act.

All of these are expectations subtly communicated to parents about expectations of how others think the child should be raised.

Expectations come from the culture in which we live. People raised in a culture are inculcated with stereotypical beliefs or expectations. For example, we often have different expectations of people based on race, ethnicity, religion, or sexual preference. We group people into categories and draw conclusions about them. We also have more subtle groupings such as: people with disabilities, people in poverty, people with limited English proficiency, ex-felons, and people who practice occupations like plumbers, electricians, teachers, attorneys, politicians, brain surgeons, garbage collectors, and so on.

One's culture also creates expectations based on peer pressure. If you do not follow the unwritten rules of your peer group, you might feel that you will be rebuked in some manner. People sometimes resort to violence to reinforce the unwritten rules/expectations. Think back to demonstrations for equal rights movements related to Women's Suffrage, Black Lives Matter, Hispanics, LGBTQ, and #MeToo.

Expectations determine your reality. They impact your daily performance. They can propel you to unbelievable success or they can bury you in the depth of despair. Once you are aware of the subtle nature of expectations, you can then control their impact on your life.

~

"Expectations determine your reality.
You decide—will they bury you or
propel you to great heights?
You get what you expect!"
Bill Blokker, EdD

~

Impact of Expectations

Some of you are skeptical about what you are reading; that's a good thing. Being skeptical provides you the opportunity to think, question, and analyze information. Whether you are a skeptic or not, here is specific research that is the foundation supporting this chapter.

In 1968, the research on expectations from Robert Rosenthal and associates highlighted the *Self-Fulfilling Prophecy*, a broad term that encompasses the following:

1. *Pygmalion Effect*—significant other's expectations of you, whether positive or negative, significantly impact your thinking and behavior.

2. *Galatea (gal-ah-tee-ah) Effect*—your expectations of yourself, whether positive or negative, significantly impacts your thinking and behavior.

Becoming aware of and understanding these effects allows you to better understand and control expectations.

Here is one study by Robert Rosenthal that focused on the Pygmalion Effect. There were a group of people who were asked to train rats to work through a maze. These trainers were told that the rats in group A had been bred to be "maze bright" and the rats in group B to be "maze dull." At the conclusion the study, the group A, "maze bright" rats outperformed the group B, "maze dull" rats.

Unbeknownst to the trainers, this study was not about "maze dull" or "maze bright" lab rats. The trainers were the real focus of the study. When Rosenthal informed the trainers about the characteristics of the two groups of rats, he set expectations in their minds. The trainers did not know that there was no difference in the intelligence of the rats. There was no special breeding or characteristics. They were all standard lab rats. As a result of this study, Rosenthal and associates concluded that the trainer's expectations of the rats impacted how they worked with them, thus causing a difference in performance of the two groups.

Similar studies of the Pygmalion Effect have been done with teachers of elementary school children and trainers in adult vocational training programs. All the studies yielded the same results. The expectations held by the superiors drove their verbal and non-verbal behavior with the subordinates to get the expected results. When superiors were told certain subordinates were more intelligent or more capable, those people outperformed the people who were labeled as lower intelligence or less capable. In all cases, researchers labeled the people in a random manner. Expectations determine your reality.

~

"The positive thinker sees the invisible,
feels the intangible and achieves the impossible."
Winston Churchill

~

Combating the Impact of Low Expectations

Expectations control your reality. When others have low expectations of you, it can have a devastating impact on your performance and mindset. Many people in our society experience low expectations from others daily.

Anyone who falls into a disenfranchised or stigmatized group experiences low expectations. This is common in all societies. In the USA, the most likely to experience low expectations are people of color, females, and low-income individuals. Consciously or subconsciously, people in these groups are often viewed by others as being incapable of performing at a high level.

If you accept others' low expectations of you, one or more of the following happens:

1. Your confidence is depressed by their lack of belief in your ability.

2. Their low expectations sabotage your efforts because:

   a. They continually communicate their doubts regarding your ability to succeed

   b. They emphasize obstacles that will hinder you

   c. They put obstacles in your way

   d. They don't provide needed time or materials for the task

   e. They don't provide any coaching to assist with overcoming obstacles.

3. You begin to focus on your obstacles rather than solutions to overcome them.

4. You put forth less intellectual effort.

5. You put forth less emotional effort.

Keep in mind that when people give you advice or communicate their expectations to you, they are doing so from their own personal perspective. Their advice comes from their own set of experiences, values, fears, knowledge, strengths, desires, needs. Their advice to you is based on *their view* of the world, *not yours!*

If the advice others give you supports what you want to do, great, give it the thought it deserves. But if the advice they offer does not support your high expectations, ask them to explain in more detail what is making them unsupportive. Ask the person to provide more than a cursory or surface-level explanation. If they can't give you more detailed information, ignore any advice they want to give you. If they provide more detailed info, listen to it and consider it. However, "considering it" does not mean you accept it; just analyze it and decide for yourself later.

Think back to the stories you read in this book about Victoria Arlen, Wilma Rudolph, and Benjamin O. Davis Jr.

Arlen and Rudolph had medical experts say they would not succeed. Davis actually had people throwing obstacles in his way so he would not succeed. All three had high expectations for themselves. They decided their expectations would rule their destiny rather than the low expectations of the others.

~

"It always seems impossible, until it is done!
Nelson Mandela

~

Here is an excellent example of combating cultural bias and low expectations of others. This person made the impossible, possible in many ways! As a result of her high expectations, she and many others achieved beyond expectations.

What would be the expectations for an African-American female born in 1918, in White Sulphur Springs, West Virginia? Because of segregation, she had to attend a "colored" school. In fact, there was no schooling available to her after eighth grade in her town. All women, but especially African-American women, had to understand "their place" in society. They were to be quiet and do as they were told.

The woman is Katherine Johnson. Even though she experienced tremendous discrimination, by age 18 Katherine graduated summa cum laude from West Virginia State University with a BS in mathematics and French. First, she became a teacher. Then she was hired by the National Advisory Committee for Aeronautics, later to become the National Aeronautics and Space Administration (NASA). In this job, she again faced unbelievable bias and low expectations:

- Federal laws required African-American women to work, eat, and use restrooms in separate facilities from the other workers.

- These women were referred to as "colored computers."

- White males were the engineers and attended all the meetings. No women were allowed in these meetings.

- Women were expected to be subservient and be quiet. Their opinions did not matter.

Johnson was determined and knew she had expertise that was needed by the all-male flight research team she was working with. She had high expectations driving her. She was assertive and said she was going to be in meetings because she was the one doing the calculations and needed to know the intricacies of the project. She quickly became highly respected by the men. Johnson became the only non-white, non-male member of the Space Task Force, charged with getting American astronauts into space as soon as possible.

She calculated the trajectory for Alan Shepard's flight. Then, NASA started using electronic computers. However, they used Johnson to verify the calculations made by the electronic computers. In fact, John Glenn refused to fly his earth orbital mission until Johnson had verified the calculations.

Because of her exceptional math expertise and contributions to the space programs, Johnson earned many prestigious awards. NASA named a building for her. In addition, she was presented with an honorary doctorate by West Virginia University. In 2015, she was awarded the Presidential Medal of Freedom. In 2016, the film *Hidden Figures* was made about her life.

Katherine Johnson accomplished her success because she refused to be controlled by expectations of others. To excel, she established her own expectations (Galatea Effect) and ignored those of the segregated, biased culture. As a result, she achieved beyond expectations and she was a significant contributor to making the impossible, possible for the astronauts. If Johnson could succeed in that situation, you can succeed in yours.

Setting High Expectations for Yourself

All the people highlighted in this book set high expectations and achieved them. They all had to overcome many obstacles. They all had many people who doubted them and told them they couldn't do what they wanted to do.

When high achievers are studied, there are five strategies they exhibit to accomplish their huge goals:

- Strategy 1: Dream Big
- Strategy 2: Use Incremental Goal Setting
- Strategy 3: Use Their Frontal Lobe to Avoid Emotion Commotion
- Strategy 4: Use Positive Self-Talk
- Strategy 5: Visualize the Dream

We are going to dig deeper into each of these five strategies to provide you with information to accomplish your high expectations.

Strategy 1: Dream Big

Challenging yourself is essential if you are going to achieve beyond expectations. So, what does the term "high expectations" mean? It means you are establishing a goal, objective, or task that makes you feel uncomfortable. It means you will push yourself to the edge of your capabilities. It means that you are willing to step outside of your comfort zone. Setting high expectations means you must suspend disbelief! You *can* make the impossible, possible!

Decide what you want your life to be. Think outside the box. Put yourself on the edge. No matter how big and grandiose, make it your goal. Write your response to these questions in your journal.

- What does it look like?
- What does it sound like?
- What does it feel like?

~

"The difference between the impossible and the possible lies in a person's determination."

Tommy Lasorda

~

Now you have high expectations of yourself. As a result of dreaming big, you have a goal that puts you on the edge, makes you feel uncomfortable. Write that goal in your journal. It must become tangible and concrete. Once you write it down, you are going to use it to drive your thinking in the next strategy.

Strategy 2: Use Incremental Goal Setting

To accomplish your big dream, you must use incremental goal setting. All the people highlighted in this book set incremental goals to enable them to achieve beyond expectations. It's like building a house. First, you build the foundation. Then you do the sub-flooring and framing. Then comes the roof, electrical, plumbing, finish work. The achievement of any goal depends on incremental steps.

If you think about it, any goal can be broken down into many smaller tasks. Just like a construction project, you can analyze the goal and break it into many individual tasks that have to get done from beginning to end.

Do a "brain dump" about any and all thoughts you have related to accomplishing your goal. No idea is too big or too small. No thought is more important than another. *Whatever pops into your brain, dump it on to a page in your journal.*

Once you have your brain dump, now you must sort out all the ideas and thoughts. Here are some categories to guide your thinking as you begin to develop your incremental steps needed to accomplish your goal. Write your response to each in your journal.

1. Knowledge/skill and tactics you need to develop
2. Experts who can assist your development of your knowledge/skill and tactics
3. Emotional control knowledge/skills you will need to develop
4. Experts who are going to assist with emotional control skill development
5. Emotional support people

Your thoughts/ideas in each of these categories are the raw material needed to create your plan to accomplish your big dream. Understand that you do not need a "perfect" plan before you begin your implementation. No matter how much you plan, there are always things that are missed in the planning process. Get a rough plan together and *get started*! Nothing happens until something happens. Action stimulates energy, solutions and success. Inertia promotes paralysis!

~

"Make incremental progress,
change comes not by the yard, but by the inch."
Rick Pitino

~

There are four key factors to keep in mind as you begin your implementation:

1. Always begin working on those incremental goals that you can accomplish quickly and easily. Then move to ones a little more challenging.

2. Seek advice from "experts" who have accomplished the same or similar goal. Discuss your process in detail with them.

3. You will continually need to monitor and adjust your steps. Expect the unexpected.

   a. Something will always come up that you have not thought about.

   b. Something will not work as expected.

4. Stay focused on solutions rather than problems. Pat yourself on the back. Take pride in what you have accomplished so far.

Here's a reality check! During this process, you will get frustrated. There will be times you think you have run into a brick wall. Understand this happens to everyone. It is not just happening to you. Anytime you attempt any change in life you will run into obstacles. When this happens, remember, execution transcends talent. What matters most in life is not what happens, but *your reaction* to what happens!

～

"Nothing is impossible. The word itself says
I M POSSIBLE."
Audrey Hepburn

～

Strategy 3: Use Your Frontal Lobe to Avoid Emotion Commotion

Unmet expectations can be a threat to your dignity. As a result, your fight/flight response is activated. You want to avoid this at all costs. When emotion commotion sets in, nothing good happens.

As you recall from chapter 3, there are multiple strategies to control your emotional reactions in any situation. You read that the frontal lobe has tremendous capacity to control your emotional reaction as well as generate many creative solutions to problems. This creative problem solving is possible *only when the brain is in a positive mindset.* When negativity sets in, it paralyzes the brain from using any function other than fight/flight.

Strategy 4: Use Positive Self-Talk

Positive self-talk is essential to accomplish your high expectations. You are putting yourself on the edge. You are pushing yourself past what you ever thought was possible.

As a result, negativity and doubt will begin to creep into your mind. This is the time that positive self-talk is critical.

Remember from what you read in prior chapters, self-talk is a form of "mind control." What you say to yourself, is what you believe. Negative self-talk has a toxic and paralyzing effect on your brain and body. Positive self-talk ignites energy and creativity that helps you achieve your high expectations.

$\sim$

"Self-talk is the most powerful form of communication because it either empowers you or it defeats you."

Wright Thurston

$\sim$

Strategy 5: Visualize the Dream

Visualization is the mental rehearsal of any activity you want to perform in real life. Visualization is a most powerful tool to fuel your quest to achieve your high expectations. Visualization helps embed the movement, thoughts, and emotions necessary to accomplish your goal.

Aymeric Guillot, PhD, a professor at the Center of Research and Innovation in Sport at University Claude Bernard, in Lyon, France, says visualization triggers the nervous system so your mental performance develops neural pathways similar to when performing the actual activity. Michael Gervais, PhD, a performance psychologist, says the most effective imagery involves as many of the five senses as possible.

World champion ice skater Brian Boitano, in his book *Boitano's Edge,* talks about how he used visualization with all of his senses to help him in his quest for an Olympic gold medal.

> *In fact, the night I won the Olympic gold medal, everything happened exactly how I had visualized it: the way I cried at the end of my program and then laughed, and the way the audience stood before I was done. I actually started thinking, "Is this real or am I visualizing it?"*
>
> *It wasn't until I was standing on the podium and the "Star Spangled Banner" began to play that I realized I had won. The music played at a faster tempo than I had visualized, and I thought, "This is too fast." Then I thought, "But this is real. It's real!"*

There is not one best way to visualize. In fact, there are many different theories about the best methods of visualization. Here are the basics. Learn them, then do what works for you.

As you visualize:

- Close your eyes.
- Relax and focus only on your goal activity.
- Mentally rehearse your actions, emotions, and thoughts needed to "participate in the performance" from beginning to end. During this mental rehearsal, use self-talk and key words to trigger the desired actions.
- Include as many of the five senses as possible during the visualization.
- Always be positive and successful.

If you are rehearsing a situation where an adversary is involved (e.g., an athletic contest, job interview, oral exam, interpersonal confrontation, etc.), your simulation should include the adversary presenting different challenging situations which you counter successfully.

World champion golfer Jack Nicklaus has said: "I never hit a shot, not even in practice, without having a very sharp in-focus picture of it in my head."

World champion ski racer Lindsey Vonn says she visualizes her run down the course hundreds of times before the actual race. During these visualizations, you will see Vonn shifting her weight back and forth as she progresses down the course, in her mind. While doing this, she also uses breathing patterns she will use during the race.

My son-in-law is a professional dancer. I have watched him and other dancers, as part of their rehearsal sessions, using visualization to develop the neural pathways to strengthen the habit patterns necessary to perform the dance with automaticity.

It is especially important that you pay attention to the emotional state during the visualization. In your real-life situation, if you anticipate a variety of problems, you must incorporate those in your visualization. You are going to mentally rehearse how you will confront these problems. As you do this, rehearse a variety of strategies to keep yourself calm and deal with the negative challenges successfully. In other words, rehearse several ways you can monitor and adjust if things are not going the way you want. Bottom line, always stay positive and in control.

"I believe that visualization is one of the most powerful means of achieving personal goals."

Harvey Mackay

~

The more realistic and the more times you visualize the accomplishment of your goal, the better. This mental rehearsal should occur multiple times during the day. Create the situation where you are experiencing, in your mind, what you will be experiencing during the real event. Remember, the purpose of this visualization is to assist in the development of your neural pathways to form habit patterns. These habits will then come into play during the real-life application so you can meet your high expectations.

Should you visualize negative events?

The answer to this question has an important impact on your personal success. Many people visualize negative events happening in their life. They continually think about all the negative things that can happen in an upcoming situation. The more you visualize negative events happening, the more likely they will occur!

This happens for two reasons. First, all the concepts of visualizing a positive event apply equally to visualizing a negative one. In other words, you are training your brain to do something negative to yourself! You're giving birth to your own problems! Stop negative visualizations.

Second, you read about the impact of low expectations. They are detrimental to high achievement. When you are visualizing negative events, you are confirming the low expectations. You are deepening your belief that you will fail! Stop negative visualizations.

~

"Don't lower your expectations to meet your performance. Raise your level of performance to meet your expectations."

Ralph Marston

~

Expectations and the Placebo Effect

We have all heard of the placebo effect. Let's take some time to delve more deeply into what is means. The placebo effect is a medical term that is synonymous with the term expectations. The National Institutes of Health states, "The placebo effect is a beneficial health outcome resulting from a person's anticipation that an intervention will help." This outcome is caused by the administration of a substance or service that has no medicinal value of any kind. In other words, people feel better even though they do not receive any "real" medicine. The placebo effect establishes an expectation of a result.

Research tells us that placebos work 30%–35% of the time! There is documented evidence that placebos cause changes in brain chemistry. Researchers have found that when people involved in pain studies receive placebos, the brain releases endorphins that relieve the pain.

Placebos work because people expect them to work. This is verified in many studies. In fact, there have been people in cancer treatment studies who lost their hair even though they were taking a placebo! They believed they would lose their hair and they did! Remember, these people were taking no substance other than a placebo, a "sugar pill."

If the brain believes it,
the brain will achieve it!

Now let's be very cautious! There is no suggestion in this text that you should be using placebos in medical situations. Those decisions are totally up to you and your doctor. Follow the advice of your doctor.

However, we can learn from the medical research. If placebos work 30%–35% of the time, it means that if the brain believes it, the brain will achieve it. When you talk to people who achieve beyond expectation, they will tell you they expected to succeed. They were going to find a way. That mindset is what releases the brain to do whatever is necessary to create success. If the brain believes it, the brain will find a way to achieve it. If you passionately expect to succeed, the chances of you succeeding are high.

Warning! The placebo effect works toward both positive and negative results. If you believe you are going to fail, your brain will find a way for you to fail. If your brain is filled with negative thoughts about anything, it will have a negative impact on your performance. Positive expectations are essential to success, whether in medicine or any other aspect of life.

~

"Whether you think you can or you
think you can't . . . you're right."
Henry Ford

~

Setting Expectations to Get the Best Out of Yourself and Others

Achieving beyond expectations is never a solitary feat. There are always others involved. They may be involved on an informal or formal basis. Informal means they can be family, friends, or others who are supporting you. Formal means the people supporting you in a professional manner. They are employees or others providing a contract service to you. Whether your support is informal or formal, all involved must have a clear understanding of the expectations you have of them as you work to accomplish your goal.

Given this information, you must look at yourself as the "leader" of your group. As an example, Victoria Arlen's mother was the leader of the group that included medical professionals and family to make the impossible, possible for Victoria.

Having this clear understanding of expectations, roles, and responsibilities will optimize everyone's thinking and behavior. Without this clarity everyone's performance will be ineffective. From research in business, education, military, and athletics we know there are five reasons people fail to accomplish lofty goals:

1. They don't know what is expected of them.

2. They don't have the knowledge or skill to meet the expectations.

3. They don't have the desire/motivation to meet the expectations.

4. They don't have the confidence to meet the expectations.

5. Once implementation begins, they don't monitor/ adjust effectively.

"Don't blame people for not meeting your
expectations; blame yourself for not giving
them enough support to succeed."

Bill Blokker, EdD

Knowing these five reasons provides direction to the leader. You must ensure that all is done to prevent them. In 1974, Ralph Stogdill, in his book *Handbook of Leadership*, identified behaviors of the leaders who were successful in all they did. Stogdill wrote about the necessity of leaders establishing clear expectations for the followers. Stogdill described this as establishing "structure."

The "structure" that leaders must create includes the following:

1. State and define what is to be accomplished: task, goal, objective, expectation.

    a. Create the vision (mental image) of the expectation. Show them "the top of the jigsaw puzzle box!" (Whenever people put together a jigsaw puzzle, they refer to the box top for a vision of the finished product to see how all the pieces fit together.) The use of a video or modeling behavior is a powerful strategy to communicate the vision. If either is not possible, the leader must paint a vivid mental picture.

    b. Discuss the positive emotional impact of accomplishing the vision. Describe the excitement, success, and pride. By doing this, you begin to create the positive mindset needed by the followers to motivate their performance.

2. State and discuss how you, the leader, will assist the followers to accomplish the expectation.

   a. Explain what coaching effort, time, money, equipment, and personnel you will provide to help the person or team accomplish the expectation. By discussing the behaviors your followers can expect of you, you show them you are committed to do whatever is necessary for their success.

   b. Explain how you, the leader, will monitor everyone's efforts and adjust leadership behavior to ensure their success. This communicates ongoing support and the determination to succeed.

3. State and discuss the behaviors you, the leader, expect of the followers as they work to accomplish the expectation.

   a. Explain what it is going to take to accomplish the expectation (focus, emotional control, persistence, intensity, planning, time, effort, technical knowledge/skill, creative problem solving, cooperation with others, money, equipment).

   b. Discuss thoughts and reactions they may experience as they are working to accomplish the expectation (how positive/negative emotions impact performance, overcoming obstacles and analysis paralysis).

To effectively establish structure as described, you need to do pre-planning and in-depth thinking about what you want to accomplish and how you're going to accomplish it. Be aware that you cannot anticipate all circumstances. However, the more complete you can be with establishing the structure, the more the group will work as a team and be successful. Most importantly, *act!* Without action nothing gets done. Spend time planning and preparing but avoid analysis paralysis at all costs.

~

"The task of the leader is to get his people
from where they are to where they have not been."

Henry Kissinger

~

Unrealistic Expectations—A Major Cause of Failure

Many people establish New Year's resolution goals. They work diligently on them for several days, then give up. They begin with lots of motivation and energy, but soon that fades away and they are defeated. They quit!

A work group begins a new project. There's a lot of energy and excitement at the beginning. However, before long, there are only a couple of people really putting effort into the project. All others have lost interest. Failure is imminent. What causes the failure?

Unrealistic expectations are a major cause of failure. The person or group does not understand the natural course of events that occur any time you embark on a major new task. People must understand the intricacies of the change process. If people have realistic expectations going into a major new project, they're better prepared to deal with the issues that arise.

In 1965, Bruce Tuckman presented a group development model. This important information is presented because it identifies a major cause of failure or poor performance when attempting to make a change. The research indicates groups and individuals *always* go through four developmental stages when they work on a new project. You cannot avoid these stages. You can shorten the amount of time spent in a specific stage, but it is not possible to completely skip a stage. If you are going to achieve beyond expectations, *you must expect to progress through these four stages and be prepared to adjust behaviors depending on the developmental stage.*

The original model had four stages of development: Forming, Storming, Norming, and Performing, as shown at the bottom of Tuckman's Developmental Stages of a Group graphic in Figure 5. Some years later, he added a fifth stage, Mourning. That fifth stage focused on what happens when the team breaks up after the task is completed. For our purposes, we will be spending all of our time discussing the first four stages.

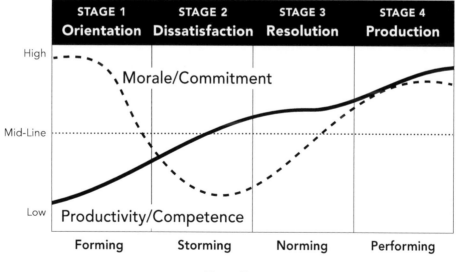

Figure 5.

Look at the dashed and solid lines going across the graph. The dashed line reveals how morale and commitment change so dramatically as people move through each stage. The solid line shows what happens to productivity and competence through each stage.

As you can see, the morale/commitment dips very quickly. This "implementation dip" is a major cause of failure in any project. The reason for the implementation dip is people come face to face with the challenges of making significant change. The change is more difficult than they had anticipated. As a result, disappointment and frustration overruns all of their positive energy. Emotion commotion sets in which can cause people to give up!

Everyone must clearly understand the challenges that always occur when implementing any change. You cannot avoid them. When you are aware that they will occur, you can develop the knowledge/skill to minimize them. The leader must be responsible to take the steps to minimize the "implementation dip.

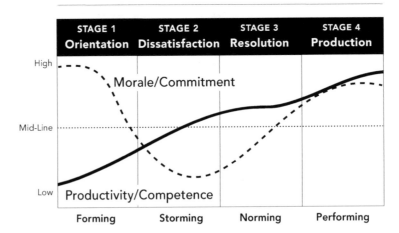

TUCKMAN'S DEVELOPMENTAL STAGES OF A GROUP

ACHIEVE BEYOND EXPECTATIONS

Here is a detailed description of the developmental stages.

Developmental Stage	Characteristics	Impact on Performance
Stage 1: Orientation – Forming	A. Excitement about the benefits of the upcoming change. B. Excitement about new task. C. Need to develop knowledge/skill. D. Questions arise about task and individual responsibilities. E. Must learn to work effectively with group members. F. As time goes on, there are more questions/problems than answers.	**Morale/Commitment** is high at the start but drops off rapidly. Reality sets in. There are knowledge/skill problems and group interaction issues. Frustration grows rapidly. Emotion commotion sets in. **Productivity/Competence** is low. People lack the knowledge and skills to do the task. Equally frustrating, they begin to have group dynamic problems and conflict.
Stage 2: Dissatisfaction – Storming	G. Knowledge/skill is developing. H. Some task goals are accomplished. I. Disagreements about task issues more prevalent. J. Questioning the importance of the task—is this worth doing? K. Frustrations grow about group working relationships. L. Power struggles within group. M. People need clarification of individual responsibilities. N. Morale and commitment to the task is in a downward spiral.	**Morale/Commitment** falls off rapidly and hits a low point. This is the "implementation dip." Emotion commotion is in complete control. This is where most people and groups quit. During this time, people start thinking the effort to accomplish the change is far greater than the potential benefits. **Productivity/Competence** is improving. It surpasses the mid-line in first half of the developmental stage. However, people are unaware of their productivity successes because morale/commitment issues are overwhelming everyone's thinking.

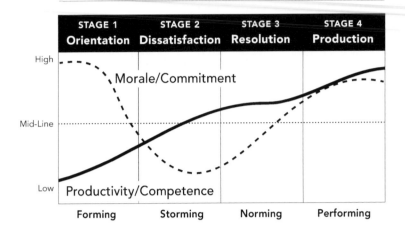

Developmental Stage	Characteristics	Impact on Performance
Stage 3: Resolution– Norming	O. People are competent and confident about skills needed to accomplish the task. P. Experiencing good productivity with task goals. Q. Group members more comfortable with their roles and responsibilities. R. Morale becoming more positive. S. Group members taking on more leadership responsibilities.	**Morale/Commitment** finally begins to improve. Emotion commotion is going away. Group members working together and resolving issues amicably. Halfway through this stage, morale/commitment rises above the midline. **Productivity/Competence** is high. People are working together. They rely on each other's expertise and understand their roles.
Stage 4: Production– Performing	T. Group roles and responsibilities established and are working effectively. U. Positive morale is evident. V. Group members demonstrating discretionary effort. W. Group taking responsibility to monitor performance and initiate adjustments as necessary. X. Productivity at the highest.	**Morale/Commitment** is high. Great team spirit. Everyone feels the success of accomplishing tasks. People put in extra effort to ensure top performance. **Productivity/Competence** is high. People are extremely knowledgeable and skilled. They work creatively to overcome obstacles to productivity.

~

"Being challenged in life is inevitable,
being defeated is optional."
Roger Crawford

~

These research-based developmental stages apply to both individuals and groups working to create any change large or small. The implementation dip is a given, but *it can be minimized* by implementing the strategies outlined in "How to Minimize the Implementation Dip."

How to Minimize the Implementation Dip

Developmental Stage	Strategies to Minimize Implementation Dip

Stage 1:
Orientation–Forming
	1. Establish "structure" (see page 184)
	   a. Clearly identify task to be accomplish.
	   b. Identify the behaviors others can expect of you, the leader, as you are working to accomplish the task–both technical knowledge/skills and emotional control skills.
	   c. Identify behaviors you expect of others as they are working to accomplish the task–both technical knowledge/skills and emotional control skills.
	   d. Use modeling behavior to inform performance.
	2. Get expert coaching for instructive, supportive feedback.

Stage 2: **Dissatisfaction–** **Storming**	3. Reinforce effective interactions and task accomplishments. 4. Remind yourself and others that this is the stage where emotion commotion can take over if all are not vigilant and applying emotional control skills. 5. Provide rationale for why others need to work in the way you are requesting. 6. Continue expert coaching and modelling as necessary. 7. Listen to and discuss issues; be "soft on the person, hard on the problem."

Developmental Stage	Strategies to Minimize Implementation Dip
Stage 3: Resolution–Norming	8. Recognize/reward both effort and task performance. 9. Encourage group members to take more responsibility. 10. Encourage group members to take initiative. 11. Listen to and collaboratively discuss issues.
Stage 4: Production– Performing	12. Expect group to facilitate and reinforce structure to accomplish task. 13. Expect group to recognize and reinforce group member efforts. 14. Listen to and discuss issues. 15. Reinforce effort and task performance.

"Few things are more important during a change event than communication from leaders who can paint a clear and confidence-inspiring vision of the future."

Sarah Clayton

Any time you begin a new project or task, or learn a new skill, the implementation dip is a given. It's just like death and taxes! Expect it. Prepare for it. That way you won't be devastated when it happens. If you're unprepared, you will experience emotion commotion that can lead to paralysis and failure. The implementation dip is the primary cause for failure. People who achieve beyond expectations know that emotional control skills are what will get them through all the tough times. The implementation dip is a tough time. Be ready for it.

In my leadership and human performance company, we made extensive use of our knowledge of Tuckman's Developmental Stages. Internally, any time we began a new project, we would discuss the developmental stages with the project leader and the group members, using the How to Minimize the Implementation Dip chart.

We would look at the graphic of the developmental stages and discuss the group characteristics and leadership behaviors for each stage. We wanted everyone to become consciously competent so they could monitor their own and the group's behavior to adjust as necessary. This planning time significantly minimized the implementation dip and increased our productivity.

Externally, our consultants applied all the same strategies when working with clients. The consultants discussed the developmental stages with the clients as described above. Finally, our consultants trained our clients in the use of these strategies when beginning any new project.

You now have a better understanding of a major cause of all failure in any new endeavor: the implementation dip. Write your responses to these questions in your journal.

1. How will you apply this information to your personal behavior?
2. How can it be useful in your family?
3. What can you do with this information in your workplace?

No one likes to be unsuccessful at a task. You now have much information to avoid a major cause of failure. The power is in your hands. How will you use it?

~

"Life's challenges are not supposed to paralyze you, they're supposed to help you discover who you are."
Bernice Johnson Reagon

~

Expectations determine your reality. Each of us has experienced challenging situations in our lives. When life hits you with a traumatic issue, how do you respond. Do you expect that you can control situations? *Or*, do you expect to be overwhelmed with the situation?

Here is a moving story to illustrate that no matter the trauma you experience, setting high positive expectations leads to making the impossible, possible. Imagine this situation:

- You are a carefree girl born in rural North Carolina.
- For 11 years you live a happy young girl's life.
- It's 1948, you're in middle school when you fall gravely ill with polio.
- You spend a year in the hospital, paralyzed from the neck down. That means you can't breathe on your own.
- Doctors predict you will die within the year.

If you were the young girl, what expectations would you have? Do you think you might have a feeling of hopelessness? Would you expect to live a full and stimulating life?

Martha Mason was the little girl in this scenario. She spent an entire year in a hospital bed, with tubes and machines keeping her alive. But Martha and her parents did not accept the dire predictions of the medical professionals. They had much higher expectations for Martha's life.

Martha made the decision to be placed in an iron lung. The iron lung was invented as a form of non-invasive breathing therapy that used air pressure to allow a patient to breathe if they couldn't breathe on their own. The machine is seven feet long and weighs 800 pounds. Essentially, it confines the patient in a metal coffin, forever. Once a patient depends on an iron lung to breathe, they are in the iron lung for life. Martha Mason spent 61 years in this iron lung! When asked if she felt confined, Martha said, "I really never give it a lot of thought." She set her own high expectations, ignoring the world's doom and gloom for her.

Her middle school teachers worked with her, visiting daily to ensure she never fell behind. She didn't. Instead, Martha Mason graduated from her high school first in her class. Later, she was transported–iron lung and all–to Wake Forest University. There she graduated first in her class, earned a Phi Beta Kappa key and graduated summa cum laude. Later, she worked as a women's rights activist.

Martha Mason's high positive expectations never faded. She wrote an autobiography, *Breath: Life in the Rhythm of an Iron Lung*. Martha hosted parties at her home, where her helpers and friends would set a table right next to her iron lung. She ran a book club, read voraciously, and had a Netflix account.

No matter your life situation, you can set high expectations for yourself. In spite of her paralysis and the iron lung, Martha Mason insisted on living exactly the kind of life she wanted. She adapted to some of the world's most catastrophic circumstances. "I wouldn't have chosen this life, certainly," she said. "But given this life, I've probably had the best situation anyone could ask for." Martha Mason rejected low expectations. By her own account she lived a full and joyous life. Martha Mason achieved beyond expectations.

~

*"The quality of our expectations
determines the quality of our action."*

Andre Godin

~

Final Thoughts on Expectations

All the research is very clear. There is no doubt that expectations determine your reality. Achieving beyond expectations is possible only when you significantly increase your self-awareness about expectations and how they determine your reality.

Holding high expectations of yourself and others is the catalyst for astounding achievement. However, you must be smart about how you go about establishing the high expectations. Once you have established the high expectation, you must establish incremental tasks that will propel you to accomplishing your lofty goal. You must have coaching to ensure you have the necessary knowledge and skills for success. Most important, you must have coaching to develop the critical emotional control skills necessary to avoid emotion commotion when the going gets tough.

5 Rules for Expectations

1. Always expect the best for yourself.

2. Create incremental steps to achieve your best.

3. Continually monitor and adjust to get your best.

4. Ignore others' low expectations of you.

5. Encourage others' dreams.

Key Points: Expectations Determine Your Reality

1. Expectations determine your reality.

2. Subtly embedded expectations control your behavior from birth to death.

3. Ignore low or negative expectations from any source.

4. High expectations are essential to achieve beyond expectations. Expect they may make you feel uncomfortable.

5. Increase your self-awareness of expectations by listening to your self-talk and recognizing when you experience negative emotions.

6. Use visualization to help accomplish your high expectations.

7. Unmet expectations can lead to emotion commotion. Use your emotion control skills to avoid emotion commotion.

8. Use incremental goals to achieve your high expectations.

9. Establish "structure" to ensure there is clarity of tasks and role expectations.

10. Initiate strategies to minimize the negative impact of the implementation dip.

∼

"What will shape your destiny?
Your dreams or your fears?"

Bill Blokker, EdD

∼

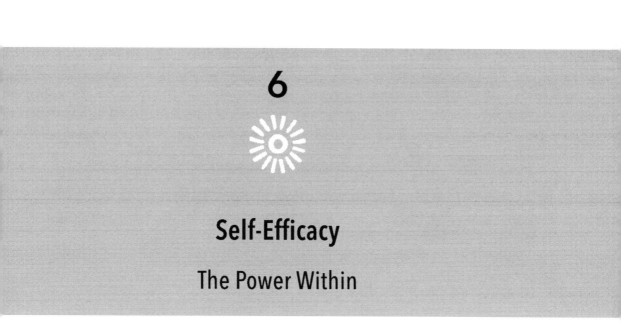

6

Self-Efficacy

The Power Within

Nearing the end of World War II, a pacifist medic named Desmond Doss found himself at the edge of a 400-foot cliff called Hacksaw Ridge. The Japanese were attempting to retake the ridge with a continuous bombardment. Doss was the only American soldier remaining on the ridge who was not dead or wounded. For hours, Doss treated wounded soldiers, carried them to the edge of the ridge, and lowered them down to medics waiting below. He did this all afternoon. One by one, soldier by soldier. He rescued 75 men that day without ever touching a gun.

You might think that being a great soldier requires violence. But Desmond Doss showed the world that keeping with your convictions could make a great soldier out of anybody, even someone who resists violence. It was truly an achievement beyond what Doss, his comrades, and his commanding officers could have ever expected. Doss was awarded the Medal of Honor along with many more meritorious awards.

HOW DID this skinny pacifist soldier manage to achieve beyond expectations? How did he make the impossible, possible? It was because of his power within, his "self-efficacy." Doss made the determination that he was going to rescue as many of his comrades as he could until he was killed himself. He persisted under unimaginable conditions. He overcame every obstacle. Even though he was totally exhausted, he persisted for hours, saving man after man, one at a time. Just think of the effort it takes to lower one man down a 400-foot cliff by yourself with people shooting at you. Doss did it 75 times!

All of us have self-efficacy, a power within. Not many of us will ever have an experience that comes close to what Doss had to do. But all of us have the same opportunity to exercise our own power within. All the same things that drove Doss to such exceptional feats are available to each of us to use however we choose. We all have the same potential. This potential resides within our brain. It is up to each of us to tap into our brain and awaken the power within.

"Self" Awareness

What is your belief in your ability to handle a difficult situation? When you are presented with a challenging task, what is your initial response? When the going gets tough, how do you respond?

These questions focus on the vision you have of your "self." Your honest answers to these questions will provide insight into how you feel about your "self." To achieve beyond expectations, you must have a foundational understanding of the single most powerful driving force that impacts you every second of every day. You must be constantly observing your "self" to determine what you can do to make your life better.

In addition to observing your "self," you must pay attention to others. You are impacted by people making decisions based on what's best for their "self." In your daily life, many of the problems you must solve are based on a conflict between what one person feels is best for her "self" and what you think is best for your "self."

~

The self is not something one finds.
It is something that one creates.
Thomas Szasz

~

The "self" is so pivotal to your daily performance that there are thousands of books written about it. Psychiatrists and psychologists refer to "self-constructs." Worldwide there are tens of thousands of people who derive their income from helping people effectively deal with their "self."

There are four terms regarding "self" that you have undoubtedly heard or discussed at some time in your life: self-image, self-esteem, self-concept, and self-confidence. These terms are topics of hundreds of research studies. There is much importance attributed to these four terms in relation to the success or failure people have in their lives.

However, since the late 1970s there is another "self" term that has been researched and written about. Professor

Albert Bandura, PhD, Stanford University, published a paper on "self-efficacy." Today, there is consensus that self-efficacy is the driving force behind all extraordinary achievement.

Self-efficacy is the belief you have in your ability to take on and successfully complete tasks no matter how large or small, simple or complex. Self-efficacy is what drives you to make the impossible, possible. As Dr. Bandura wrote:

> Among the mechanisms of human agency, none is more central or pervasive than people's beliefs in their efficacy to influence events that affect their lives. This core belief is the foundation of human inspiration, motivation, performance accomplishments, and emotional well-being. Unless people believe they can produce desired effects by their actions, they have little incentive to undertake activities or to persevere in the face of difficulties. Whatever other factors serve as guides and motivators, they are rooted in the core belief that one has the power to affect changes by one's actions. This core belief operates through its impact on cognitive, motivational, affective, and decisional processes.

In short, *self-efficacy is the power within you*. It is your belief in your ability to succeed in a challenging situation. If you believe you will be successful in a situation, you will find a way to succeed. You will do whatever it takes. You will be creative. You will be resilient. You will persist until you succeed. If you do not believe you will be successful, you will fail!

There have been many self-efficacy studies since Badura's original work. All of them reinforce Bandura's statement that, "self-efficacy is the foundation of all human inspiration, motivation, performance accomplishments, and emotional well-being." In other words, we each have the power within to do great things. But we must know how to develop that self-efficacy within ourselves.

One is not born with self-efficacy. It is a learned behavior. That's why not everyone has the same amount of it. Indeed, there is a significant difference in characteristics of people relative to their belief in their ability to accomplish a difficult task. People who make the impossible, possible, have a high level of self-efficacy. They believe they will find a way to achieve their goals. What about you? Look at the table below; as you read the items, think about whether you end up more on the left side or the right side.

People lacking self-efficacy tend to:	People who are self-efficacious are:
• be pessimistic • be focused on problems • be unwilling to take risks • believe they will be unsuccessful with a task • give up easily when obstacles arise	• optimistic • focused on solutions • willing to take risks • trust they will be successful with a task • resilient; they persist no matter the obstacles they may face

~

"Impossible is just a big word thrown around by small men who find it easier to live in the world they've been given than to explore the power they have to change."
Muhammad Ali

~

How to Determine Your Level of Self-Efficacy

In 1992, Professors Ralf Schwarzer and Matthias Jerusalem created The General Self-Efficacy Scale, which has become the most popular self-efficacy scale. Since its creation, it has been referenced in hundreds of articles regarding self-efficacy. Here's how to use it. Read each statement, then in your journal, record the number in the column for each statement that best describes you.

General Self-Efficacy Scale[1]

Statement	Not at all true	Hardly true	Moderately true	Exactly true
I can always manage to solve difficult problems if I try hard enough.	1	2	3	4
If someone opposes me, I can find the means and ways to get what I want.	1	2	3	4
It is easy for me to stick to my aims and accomplish my goals.	1	2	3	4
I am confident that I could deal efficiently with unexpected events.	1	2	3	4
Thanks to my resourcefulness, I know how to handle unforeseen situations.	1	2	3	4
I can solve most problems if I invest the necessary effort.	1	2	3	4
I can remain calm when facing difficulties because I can rely on my coping abilities.	1	2	3	4
When I am confronted with a problem, I can usually find several solutions.	1	2	3	4
If I am in trouble, I can usually think of a solution.	1	2	3	4
I can usually handle whatever comes my way.	1	2	3	4

[1] Schwarzer, R., & Jerusalem, M. (1995). Generalized Self-Efficacy scale. In J. Weinman, S. Wright, & M. Johnston, Measures in health psychology: A user's portfolio. Causal and control beliefs (pp. 35-37). Windsor, England: NFER-NELSON.

Interpreting Your Results

Total all the numbers you have recorded in your journal. The score on this scale reflects the strength of an individual's *generalized* self-efficacy belief. The higher the score, the greater is the individual's *generalized* sense of self-efficacy. The highest score possible is 40. In a study done in the United States, the average score for 1,594 adults was 29.48.

You may or may not be happy with your score. If you are satisfied, take time to analyze what you believe to be your behaviors or habits that cause you to be self-efficacious. If you are unhappy with your score, the good news is that the remainder of this chapter will provide you with a multitude of strategies to develop your self-efficacy.

Helping Others Develop Self-Efficacy

Note that if you are in any type of leadership position—be it as an executive, director, supervisor, manager, teacher, youth leader, pastor, or coach—you can use all the information in this chapter to guide the people you lead. By developing their self-efficacy skills, they will significantly increase their ability to overcome challenges they experience.

If you are a parent, this information is also invaluable for teaching and modeling self-efficacy with your children. Life is a series of challenges. The more self-efficacious your children, the more successful they will be.

Developing Your Self-Efficacy

Dr. Bandura attributes the development of self-efficacy to four sources of influence:

- Mastery experiences (develop expertise—knowledge, skill and tactics)
- Vicarious experiences provided by social models (learn from modeling behavior)
- Social persuasion (expert coaching to improve performance)
- Interpreting emotional states (understanding and controlling emotions)

The development of your self-efficacious behavior will be accelerated by applying Bandura's four sources of influence in your daily life.

Mastery Experiences (Develop expertise– knowledge, skills, tactics)

To succeed in any task or challenge, one needs to develop expertise in the technical knowledge, skills, and tactics necessary to successfully complete a task or objective. Mastery experience means you:

- have superior technical knowledge/skill regarding a subject/task;
- practice for extended time to perfect your craft;
- continually analyze your performances and learn from both your mistakes and successes;
- perform at a subconscious level in a superior manner;
- develop the neural pathways, that allow you to function at a subconscious level in stressful situations.

The result: you can perform tasks, at a superior level, at will.

~

"What lies behind us and what lies before us are small matters compared to what lies within us."

Ralph Waldo Emerson

~

Mastery experience causes you to become consciously competent about all aspects of the behavior needed to accomplish your task/skill. When you are consciously competent, you learn:

- what works and the specific mindset or behaviors that cause it to work;
- what doesn't work and the specific mindset and behaviors that cause the problem;
- to identify and implement creative solutions to resolve the problems.

As you are working to become consciously competent, expect to feel some disappointment or frustration. This is normal. Whenever you are learning new behaviors, there is always going to be a "trial-and-error" period. This is unavoidable. It always happens. However, avoid wallowing in the mistakes or problems. Use disappointment as a trigger to initiate another effort to learn what will work successfully. Because of this trial-and-error learning, you will slowly become more and more successful. Mistakes are minimized or eliminated. This mastery experience process is lengthy. It is essential that you are persistent and maintain a positive focus.

Vicarious Experiences Provided by Social Models (Learn from modeling behavior of experts)

This terminology simply means that you create occasions to observe experts successfully modeling the task/skill you want to perform. Through that modeling process, you develop a vision of the intricacies of a mastery performance. This is then your guide as you refine your performance. Watching videos demonstrating the behaviors you want to master is equally powerful. Athletes and actors have been using this technique for years.

It is also important to see how your expert role models handle it when the performance is less than perfect. By observing their trial-and-error process, you learn how the role models monitor and adjust their performance to compensate for a less-than-acceptable effort. Observing this helps develop your own vision for how you should overcome obstacles when they occur for you.

If you can do more than observe your expert role models, such as actually having conversations with them, the learning is even better. If you get this opportunity, make use of it; pick their brains. Find out what they are truly thinking when things go well and when they don't. Your personal interaction is likely to provide the most significant insight into the mastery experience.

$\sim$

"Life is full of challenges, but we can always
find alternative ways of approaching our difficulties,
which will often lead to new discoveries."
Dame Evelyn Glennie

$\sim$

Social Persuasion (Expert constructive coaching to improve performance)

Social persuasion is when a coach, mentor, counselor, teacher, parent, advisor, or guru provides you with constructive information to improve your technical performance or provides emotional support. Whatever this person is called, her primary goal is to create a consciously competent performer who possesses a high degree of self-efficacy. This coach has the expertise to successfully guide you through the challenges that you will experience on your quest for mastery.

Coaching responsibilities fall into two areas:

- provide expert advice regarding the technical knowledge, skill, and tactics needed to consistently perform a task at a mastery level

- provide expert advice regarding the emotional control skills needed to consistently perform at a mastery level

Interpreting Emotional States (Understanding and controlling emotions)

Self-efficacious people understand and control strong emotions by using their frontal lobe. They know that nothing good happens when emotion commotion sets in. Strong emotions, whether positive or negative, can be paralyzing. Strong emotions can destroy logical thinking. How you interpret and react to your emotional state is critical to your success. For example, when an unexpected obstacle rears its ugly head, how do you react to it? Here are two different interpretations you could have:

1. "This is too big and complex and there is no way to overcome it."

2. "This is going to be an interesting challenge. I know I can find a way around this."

The first reaction effectively ends your quest for high achievement. It causes you to begin the process of failing. The second reaction continues the quest for success. It encourages you to be resilient and get into a problem-solving mode. Your interpretation of the situation is of paramount importance. Obstacles to success are a way of life. They cannot be avoided. They will pop up at the most inconvenient times. Staying positive and focused on solutions is what makes the impossible, possible.

*What matters in life is not what happens, but **your reaction** to what happens.* Whenever obstacles appear, your interpretation of the situation sets the stage for success or failure. It is critical to interpret challenges as learning situations.

To consistently achieve at a high level, one must train the frontal lobe to control emotions in challenging situations. Self-efficacious people know they must maintain a positive and optimistic mindset no matter the challenges they face. This mindset allows the brain to work to its full potential to solve problems.

∽

"Optimism is the faith that leads to achievement.
Nothing can be done without hope and confidence."

Helen Keller

∽

Strategies to Develop Bandura's Four Sources of Influence

To achieve beyond expectations, you must apply Bandura's four sources of influence to your daily activities. Here is a table of specific strategies to guide your application.

Source of Influence	Strategies to Develop Your Self-Efficacy
Mastery Experiences: becoming consciously competent about all aspects of your performance	1. Set a specific goal that you will achieve. 2. Determine what technical knowledge/skills are needed to achieve the goal 3. Using information from #2 above, do a self-assessment regarding what knowledge/skills you have at present and what you need to accomplish the goal. 4. Through multiple "trial-and-error" activities learn the new knowledge/skills. Constantly analyze successes and missteps to determine what and why things work and don't work. This will cause you to be consciously competent. 5. You must remain focused, positive, and persistent over time. Understand it is going to take time to accomplish the goal. 6. Daily growth/development is essential. Satisfaction with existing performance leads to complacency.
Vicarious Experiences: provided by social models: create a vision for success by observing expert performances	7. Identify others who are performing in the manner you desire to perform. 8. Observe them and analyze what they do and how they do it. If possible, have conversations with them to learn from their expertise. 9. Watch videos of performances related to your goal behavior; these are powerful tools to create the visual model of success in your brain. 10. Continually compare your "trial-and-error" effort from #4 above to the vision you have of the expert performing in the way you want to perform.

Source of Influence	Strategies to Develop Your Self-Efficacy

Social Persuasion: expert constructive coaching to improve performance	11. Get instructive, positive coaching to develop:
	   a. Technical knowledge/skill/expertise related to the goal to be achieved
	   b. Emotional control skills and support to maintain positive focus and persistence
	
	12. You may need two different coaches to accomplish #11 above. A knowledge/skill coach and an emotional coach. If there are two coaches, it is essential they have a common vision of what is needed and sustain a coordinated effort.
	
	13. The coach continually works to cause the performer to become consciously competent about what causes the desired behavior–both knowledge/skill and emotional control.
	
	14. The coach must understand how to apply different coaching techniques depending on the developmental stage of the performer (Review Tuckman's Developmental Stages on page 187).

Interpreting Emotional State: ability to understand and control your emotions	15. Learn how to control your emotions rather than your emotions controlling you (see chapter 3, "Avoid Emotion Commotion"). 16. Understand that emotional control is an ongoing, never-ending process. 17. Every misstep has the potential to paralyze the entire effort if you chose to wallow in your lack of success. 18. Look at every challenge or setback as a learning opportunity. It is a way to demonstrate your resilience and expertise.

Application Example of Bandura's Four Sources of Influence

Now, let's take this one step further and look at a real-life application of these self-efficacious activities. We will use Dr. Roger Bannister as our example. In 1954, Bannister was going to attempt to run a mile in under four minutes. To be the first person to run the mile that fast, he had to overcome huge psychological and physical obstacles. Bannister was going to make the impossible, possible! Here is a brief description of the challenge and what he did to achieve his goal, as sourced from a variety of public documents found in my research of his efforts.

~

"Think big and don't listen to people who tell you it can't be done. Life is too short to think small."

Tim Ferriss

~

Roger Bannister was a full-time medical student in his final year of residency. He was spending long hours each day in the classroom and hospital. His training to break the four-minute mile record was limited to time he had available at his lunch hour, for 45–60 minutes per day.

There was much debate and publicity leading up to Bannister's attempt. Here is a sampling of the atmosphere:

- World experts in track, medicine, and physics said it was impossible.

- Medical doctors said Bannister would die of oxygen deprivation because of putting such stress on his body to run that fast.

Bannister had a high level of self-efficacy. He expected to be successful. He didn't see the four-minute mile as an impossible dream. He was obsessed with being the first person to run a mile in under four minutes. It was his driving passion.

Working with his coach, Franz Stampfl, Bannister, along with two teammates, were doing new experimental workouts called interval training. They ran excruciatingly fast intervals. They practiced their pace-setting. They strategized. Finally, the day came. In a track meet on May 6, 1954, in front of three thousand spectators in Oxford, England, Roger Bannister attempted the impossible.

During the race, one teammate led for half the distance, just as they'd practiced. Then another teammate kept the pace for the next quarter mile. Then Bannister took off. After months of training, research, and preparation, Bannister forced his body to give him its absolute maximum effort. His body had nothing left to give. When he crossed the finish line, he lost consciousness.

The announcer took his time before announcing the result, letting the drama in the crowd build. The crowd exploded into screams when the announcer began with "three" and the rest was drowned out entirely. Bannister had run the mile in 3:59.4 (3 minutes, 59 and 4-tenths seconds).

Bannister and his teammates had done it. Three students at Oxford University chose to achieve beyond expectations and attempt a feat that the brightest minds in the world believed would kill them. Their self-efficacy and perspiration literally changed what scientists believed was possible for human beings.

Today, the mile record is an otherworldly 3:43 (3 minutes, 43 seconds). But still, the four-minute barrier that Bannister and his teammates shattered that afternoon is legendary. They were students and amateurs who made the impossible, possible!

~

"All our dreams can come true if we
have the courage to pursue them."

Walt Disney

~

If we compare Roger Bannister's accomplishment with Bandura's four sources of influence, we can see many parallels. First, there was no doubt in Bannister's mind that he could accomplish his goal. He believed it was going to happen; he just needed to find a way to make it happen no matter what circumstances might arise to knock him off course. Here is what was reported regarding Bannister's thinking, training, and statements. We will compare these to Bandura's four sources of influence.

Source of Influence	Examples of Self-Efficacious Behavior
Mastery Experiences: becoming consciously competent about all aspects of your performance	1. Bannister had a specific goal that he believed he could achieve: run a mile under four minutes. 2. He did research on the mechanics of running to determine the best mechanical model to accomplish his goal. 3. His coach, Fritz Stampfl, had him using a "scientific training" method, interval training. 4. The interval training allowed him to have intense workouts in a short amount of time. 5. He was continually self-assessing regarding what knowledge/skills he had and what more he needed to develop to accomplish the goal. 6. Medically he knew that his leg length, lung capacity, and "slow-twitch" muscle cells gave him a distinct advantage over other competitors. 7. Through trial and error he pushed himself to learn new skills (speed training). He was constantly analyzing his successes and missteps to become consciously competent about what worked and what needed to be changed. 8. He understood that this was going to take a long time to accomplish (12–18 months). He was persistent and focused over time. 9. He understood that he had to improve a little bit each day. He was never satisfied with existing performances.

Source of Influence	Examples of Self-Efficacious Behavior
Vicarious Experiences provided by social models: create a vision for success by observing expert performances	10. From his other race experience, Bannister realized that it was possible to run under the four-minute barrier. He had come within three seconds of the goal during two races. 11. "There was a real urgency to break the record in 1954," Bannister told *USA Today* in 1994. "It was clear that (Australian) John Landy or (American) Wes Santee would break it soon if I didn't get there first."
Social Persuasion: expert constructive coaching to improve performance	12. Franz Stampfl coached Roger Bannister using "scientific methods" (interval training and speed training). 13. Stampfl convinced Bannister that he could accomplish his goal. In fact, Stampfl said he could run a mile in 3 minutes 56 seconds. 14. Chris Chataway and Chris Brasher were Bannister's training partners and pacers during the race. They provided strong encouragement to him. 15. The day of the race, Stampfl told Bannister that despite the weather, he should give it his best try, saying, "If you don't take this opportunity, you may never forgive yourself." 16. At the end of the race, Bannister, Brasher, and Chataway grabbed one another and celebrated: "We have done it, the three of us!"
Interpreting Emotional State: ability to understand and control your emotions	17. Bannister said, "I knew enough medicine and physiology to know it wasn't a physical barrier, but it was a psychological barrier . . . As it became clear that somebody was going to be able to do it, I decided that I would prefer it to be me." 18. Bannister talked of learning to channel the body's energy, mental and physical, into a few decisive moments on the track. 19. Bannister experienced several races where he performed poorly. He used these to trigger more intense training. 20. A month before the record attempt Bannister was feeling "stale" so he decided to take three days off to go hiking and clear his head.

Roger Bannister achieved beyond expectations. He made the impossible, possible. Bannister led the way through the sub-four-minute mile psychological barrier. Because of his self-efficacious behavior, he opened the doors to many others. Within four years after Bannister broke the four-minute mark, 16 others also ran sub-four-minute miles.

∼

"Act as if you are the person you want to be."
Bernie Siegel

∼

Expand Your Self-Efficacy Skills

In 2008, Bandura wrote, "An Agentic Perspective on Positive Psychology."[1] In it, he discusses those characteristics that enhance self-efficacy. Bandura reports that people achieve success by learning from their unsuccessful efforts. He indicates that self-efficacious people treat failures as learning opportunities. They have an intense desire to "find a way" to succeed. The mindset of "find a way" causes them to:

- develop resilience;
- use creative higher-level thinking skills;
- develop intrinsic motivation;
- develop an internal locus of control.

---

[1] Bandura, A. (2008). An Agentic Perspective on Positive Psychology. In S. J. Lopez (Ed.), Positive Psychology: Exploring the best in people. Volume I (pp. 167-196). Wesport, CT: Greenwood Publishing Company.

Because these characteristics are so important to your efforts to make the impossible, possible, we are going to provide you how-to strategies to apply to your behavior.

Developing Resilience

The word resilience is derived from a Latin word meaning "to bounce back" or "to recoil." Like a spring, your resilience drives you to try and try again. Having resilience is a force of determination to continue your efforts to accomplish a task even if you have experienced significant setbacks. It is the Phoenix rising from the ashes. Resilient people understand that the more difficult/complex the task, the more bounce backs will be needed to accomplish it. Those who achieve beyond expectations have the highest levels of resilience.

~

"I don't measure a man's success by how high he climbs but how high he bounces when he hits bottom."

George S. Patton

~

It is easy to say that you need to be resilient. But to learn to become resilient, you need to have a vision of what resilience looks like—concrete examples of thoughts, emotions, and actions. There are six major characteristics of resilient people. Each are described in the chart. As you read them, compare the qualities to yourself. How many are descriptive of your behavior?

Resilience Characteristics

Characteristic	Behaviors

Self-Awareness	1. Continually monitoring:
	   a. personal thoughts, emotions and actions
	   b. other's actions/statements essential to the task
	2. Recognize when existing thinking/actions are not getting desired results

Goal Focus/ Commitment	3. A well-defined goal and plan of action is understood by all 4. The goal is the driving force behind all thoughts/actions 5. Possible distractions from the goal are eliminated or minimized 6. Visualize yourself accomplishing the goal 7. Practice, practice, practice the skills necessary to accomplish the goal
Emotional Control	8. Recognize that emotion commotion distracts from the goal focus 9. Emphasize the importance of a positive, optimistic mindset for all as they work to accomplish the goal 10. Celebrate small successes as they help maintain the optimistic momentum 11. Expectation of success drives all thinking
Action Oriented	12. Mindset of "nothing happens until something happens" 13. Begin with small, easily accomplished steps; this develops momentum to overpower obstacles 14. Create a sense of urgency by having firm timelines for accomplishment of all tasks 15. Expect action, then reaction rather than perfection 16. Understand that making mistakes is better than analysis paralysis
Creative Problem Solver	17. Focus on the real problem rather than the symptoms 18. Focus on how to make things happen 19. Embrace change; setbacks will tell you what is not working—learn from them 20. Solicit ideas from all those working with you 21. Seek expert advice

Tenacious	22.	Your mindset is, we *will* find a way to succeed
	23.	Setbacks are expected
	24.	Every setback stimulates greater creativity
	25.	Setbacks generate more energy
	26.	All-consuming resolve to succeed no matter how long it takes

Resilience requires all six of these characteristics. This means that when you are in a challenging situation and you feel like giving up, you must decide which of these characteristics is lacking or not functioning to its maximum. You must monitor the situation and analyze the cause of the problem. Are you lacking awareness? Or is it your goal focus or commitment? Maybe it's emotional control. Perhaps analysis paralysis has set in. Maybe, you need be more creative in your problem solving. Or you just need to *will yourself* to succeed.

The more often you act on the six characteristics of resilience, the more they will become internalized. You will develop the neural pathways to create habitual behavior. As a result, you will automatically go through a mental checklist of what you need to do if you're having trouble overcoming an obstacle. The bottom line is, you are developing the habit patterns to bounce back as many times as necessary to accomplish your goal.

~

"The greatest glory in living lies not in never falling,
but in rising every time we fall."

Nelson Mandela

~

Creative Higher-Level Thinking Skills

Whenever anyone is making a change in life, they are going to run into problems. Some problems are easily resolved; others simply do not have standard solutions that work. This is a tipping point that separates the self-efficacious person from the average person. The average person gives up. The self-efficacious person says, "I'm going to find a way to solve this problem." This mindset triggers a set of creative higher-level thinking skills that can identify strategies for the resolution of the problem.

What do we mean by creative higher-level thinking skills? In 1956, Benjamin Bloom researched and wrote extensively about what he determined to be six levels of thinking. His work became known as Bloom's Taxonomy. These levels of thinking provide a progression to be followed when learning a new skill or solving a problem.

Bloom's Taxonomy was originally developed for use in education. However, this taxonomy applies across all walks of life. Patrick Maggitti, PhD, is dean of the Villanova School of Business. He and many other business school deans agree that creative problem solving is the most important attribute for success in the business world. Dr. Maggitti says solutions to 21st century problems require these creative problem-solving skills. These are a combination of three skills: critical thinking, ability to analyze data to make quality decisions, and the ability to challenge the status quo.

Bandura, Bloom, and Maggitti all document the importance of developing creative higher-level thinking. The following chart describes Bloom's Taxonomy. Each level is dependent on the one preceding it. You cannot skip a level. Your ability to think at the higher levels requires the knowledge and skills you gain at the lower levels.

Bloom's Taxonomy—Levels of Thinking

Level of Thinking	Concept	Typical Behaviors
Knowledge ↓	• acquiring basic information • facts • fundamentals • basic processes • terminology • specific details	copy, define, describe, discover, examine, label, list, locate, match, memorize, name, observe, recite, repeat, reproduce, retell, retrieve
Understanding ↓	• construct meaning • integration of knowledge • conceptualize • classify/categorize • discuss theories and models • explain processes	classify, compare, contrast, convert, describe, differentiate, explain, extend, generalize, infer, interpret, predict, summarize, translate
Application ↓	• make use of the knowledge/concepts • implement content gained at previous levels • execute procedures • make use of skills/techniques	act, apply, complete, compute, construct, demonstrate, develop, employ, establish, examine, illustrate, manipulate, operate, practice, produce, solve, simulate, teach, use
Analysis ↓	• break into parts • determine how parts interact • differentiate • determine cause/effect • troubleshoot	break down, classify, conclude, connect, correlate, dissect, distinguish, divide, order, organize, prioritize, question, separate, subdivide, test
Evaluation ↓	• establish criteria to make judgments • make judgments • justify a position	appraise, argue, assess, check, choose, conclude, convince, criticize, critique, debate, defend, grade, judge, justify, measure, persuade, rate, rank, recommend, value
Synthesis ↓	• create new meaning • reorganize to use in different manner • create new material/process	adapt, amalgamate, anticipate, collaborate, combine, compose, create, design, formulate, hypothesize, imagine, intuit, invent, modify, originate, rearrange, rewrite

ACHIEVE BEYOND EXPECTATIONS

Analysis, Evaluation and Synthesis are considered the higher level thinking skills. These skills rely on experience gained from all the preceding levels. Higher levels of thinking are indicative of higher levels of expertise and mastery.

Using these higher-level thinking skills generates creative solutions for problems. When something is not going the way you want, you must seek more inventive and creative solutions. These three skills cause you to "think outside the box" to solve your problem.

~

"Our world as we have created it is a product
of our thinking. It cannot be changed
without changing our thinking."
Albert Einstein

~

Thinking at the higher levels of Bloom's Taxonomy is a learned skill. When you are first learning to think this way, it is done at the conscious level. As I was learning this in my early years in business, I had a printed copy of Bloom's Taxonomy taped to the wall at eye level above my desk. Whenever I was working through a challenging situation, I would refer to it. By doing this, it triggered ideas for potential solutions.

When you have been consciously thinking at these levels for many years, it becomes a habit. It becomes automatic. You develop the habit of thinking at the analysis, evaluation, and synthesis level. Thinking at this level helps you make the impossible, possible.

As you are developing or refining your ability to think at these higher levels, it is important to be aware of how emotions impact your ability to do so. Negative emotion is common when facing a problem that has resisted all of your attempts at resolution.

As you read in chapter 3, strong emotions paralyze your brain. They prevent your brain from working at its optimum. It is essential to be aware of your mindset as you are trying to overcome any challenge. If emotion commotion is present, you are *unable* to think at higher levels!

How are you going to develop your ability to think at the analysis, evaluation, and synthesis levels? You must consciously plan and work at the development of these thinking habits. As with the development of any habit pattern, it is going to take time. You will have your ups and downs. Set your goal to do it. Be patient. Be persistent. Monitor and adjust. It will pay huge dividends.

$\sim$

"If I have the belief that I can do it,
I shall surely acquire the capacity to do it
even if I may not have it at the beginning."
Mahatma Gandhi

$\sim$

Intrinsic Motivation

There are two types of motivation discussed in the research on self-efficacy: intrinsic and extrinsic. Intrinsic motivation comes from within. It is the self-generated desire to do something. Extrinsic motivation comes from an outside source. It is generated by another person or situation.

Intrinsic and extrinsic motivation are driven by rewards. Over the past decades, there has been considerable research and debate as to the impact of extrinsic and intrinsic rewards on behavior. Our discussion will focus on the areas of general agreement in that research. Overall, the bottom line is, the use of both extrinsic and intrinsic rewards is productive, if each is used in the proper manner.

~

"The way positive reinforcement is carried out is more important than the amount."

B. F. Skinner

~

Extrinsic motivation is generated by the potential of extrinsic rewards. These rewards recognize a desired behavior or trigger a desired behavior. Typical forms of extrinsic rewards are:

- verbal/non-verbal praise;
- certificates of recognition, awards, celebrations;
- loyalty programs;
- commissions/bonuses.

The first two are used to recognize effective behavior. The last two are used to trigger desired behavior.

Extrinsic motivation is dependent on the perceived value of the extrinsic reward by the potential recipient. If there is no perceived value, the behavior will not be reinforced, or the desired new behavior will not be triggered. In addition, over time, new and better rewards will be needed to reinforce or stimulate the desired behavior.

Intrinsic motivation is generated from within by intrinsic rewards. These rewards result from people analyzing their behavior and concluding they are doing well. These positive feelings are developed because of the following:

- a sense of self-achievement
- growing competence—increasing one's knowledge/skill set and productivity
- belief in the importance of the work you are doing
- a feeling of ownership in the work—you have decision-making authority
- increased task responsibilities
- satisfaction gained from improved job performance

Taking time to monitor your progress is essential. When you monitor progress, always spend time focusing on the positives that have occurred and what caused them to happen. By doing this, the positive thoughts and emotions you have will trigger the sense of an intrinsic reward. You will increase the intensity of your self-efficacy by:

- making yourself more aware of progress you have made;
- recognizing how you have grown as you work through changes in your life.

Positive feelings are also developed when a coach causes the trainee to step back and analyze a successful performance. Although an exterior person is triggering this process, it helps foster an awareness within the person about something she may not have recognized in the past. This self-recognition then creates the intrinsic reward.

Intrinsic rewards are a powerful motivator and they are addicting. People take pride in accomplishing a task into which they have put their heart and soul. This stimulates them to reach for even higher goals. This feeling of owner-ship motivates them to perform at their best.

In my company, we were continually monitoring prog-ress on challenging tasks. We always made a point of hav-ing our consultants identify specific behaviors that were responsible for the successes they achieved. By doing this, the consultants became consciously competent and their self-efficacy grew.

Intrinsic rewards are the most powerful force driving self-efficacy. Not only do they generate intrinsic motivation, they also cause you to be consciously competent. When you analyze your behavior, you learn which behaviors generate the desired results. You also learn what behaviors are not successful, so you adjust to get the desired result. This is the process that causes you to become consciously competent.

$\sim$

"Intrinsic motivation is conducive to creativity.
Extrinsic motivation is detrimental to creativity."
Daniel H. Pink

$\sim$

Develop an Internal Locus of Control

Internal locus of control was first discussed in 1954, by Julian Rotter, to identify a belief a person has regarding what controls events in his life. When people have an inter-nal locus of control, they believe they always have options available to them to make a situation better. They believe that they either control the situation or control their reac-tion to a situation.

The Locus of Control Continuum, identifies two extremes of control. At the external end, people take no responsibility for any of their behavior. They attribute their behavior to something others have pushed them to do. Or they attribute their behavior to bad/good luck or circumstances. At the internal end, people take full responsibility for their actions. They recognize they are in control of all of their behavior. Positive or negative results are always driven by what they say or do.

Locus of Control Continuum

|————————————————|————————————————|

External Locus of Control
Praises or blames external
factors outside of themselves
for results.

Internal Locus of Control
Believes their decisions and
behavior determine the
results they get in life.
No other factors are
responsible.

This is a continuum; therefore, people will be scattered at various spots along it based on:

- knowledge/skill level

- emotional control skills

- ability to monitor and adjust

- creative problem-solving capabilities

An internal locus of control is developed when you do all the following:

- implement Bandura's four sources of influence

- develop resilience

- use creative higher-level thinking skills

- use intrinsic motivation

There are several assessment tools available to determine a person's locus of control. The Duttweiler Internal Control Index is one that is considered reliable and valid (see https://fellrnr.com/wiki/Internal_Control_Index).

If you decide to use the assessment, you will get a score indicating your locus of control. This score is *not* a permanent fixed number that sticks to you the rest of your life. This number indicates where you are at the time you took the assessment. If you take the assessment in a year, you can get a very different number.

~

"You were not born a winner and you were not born a loser. You are what you make yourself to be."

Lou Holtz

~

Here is an example of locus of control. Two students take the same test in a high school history class. The next day the students get the results of the test. Both have received a failing grade! Here is how each student responds.

Student 1: "OMG! I know I didn't put much effort into studying for this, but I thought I knew enough to pass. I'd better pay more attention in class and put in more study effort for the next one."

Student 2: "You gotta be kidding me! Half the questions were stuff we never covered in class. Also, there were two trick questions that were designed to cause us to fail. The teacher sucks!"

The locus of control in each student is obvious. One is taking full responsibility for the results while the other is taking no responsibility.

It can be frustrating or even painful to have an internal locus of control. You have no excuses! If things don't go well, it is all on you. It hurts because we all want to feel good about ourselves.

When people with an external locus of control experience "failure," they make themselves feel better by claiming circumstances or others are at fault in some way. They take no responsibility.

Really what they are doing is trying to protect their already fragile ego. Unfortunately, this leads to a "victim-like" mentality. With this approach to life, these people are powerless to make significant changes. They are continually living a "woe is me" life. To make significant change in your life, you must first acknowledge that you are where you are in life as a result your decisions and behavior.

Many people will argue that you can't control everything that happens to you in life. That is totally accurate. Negative things happen through no fault of your own. For example, I know of a woman who had breast cancer. There was no evidence of breast cancer in her family. There was no evidence that she behaved in any manner that could have caused the breast cancer. There was no evidence that she could have prevented the disease. In other words, she had no responsibility for getting breast cancer.

The important point in this example is how she reacted when she was informed of the diagnosis. She had an internal locus of control. She made the decision, along with her family, that they were going to fiercely fight and beat the cancer. She exhibited a powerful internal locus of control and she was successful. What matters in life is not what happens, *but your reaction* to what happens!

Life happens to all of us. We will all experience unpleasant and challenging situations for which we have no responsibility. How we respond to these situations is what matters. You can be defeated, or you can take charge. It is your choice.

~

"Believe it can be done. When you believe something can be done, really believe, your mind will find the ways to do it. Believing a solution paves the way to solution."

David J. Schwartz

~

Habitual Thinking Patterns That Lead to Internal Locus of Control

When people have an internal locus of control, they believe they always have options to control or make a situation better. The characteristics of people with an internal locus of control are:

- Confidence in their ability to accomplish tasks (positive mindset)

- Willing to attempt tasks that others view as high risk

- Action oriented

- Generates creative alternative strategies when unsuccessful with a task

- Persistent effort to be successful

You must develop a state of mind and a way of thinking that becomes habitual. The state of mind is: "I will succeed. I will find a way." The habitual thinking patterns follow this process:

1. Set a goal.

2. Establish a plan to accomplish the goal.

3. Implement the plan.

4. Determine what worked and what needs to be adjusted.

5. Identify strategies to reinforce successes.

6. Identify alternative strategies to correct the setbacks.

7. Make another attempt.

8. Repeat the process until the goal is accomplished.

These habitual thinking patterns cause you to analyze events to determine the causes of both successes and failures. What makes the difference is your mindset: "I will be successful. I will find a way." Your passion to succeed is the blowtorch that burns through the obstacles you will encounter.

◠

"Passion is what gives meaning to our lives.
It's what allows us to achieve success
beyond our wildest imagination."

Henry Samueli

◠

Here is a story about a woman whose self-efficacy made the impossible, possible! As you will see, her life became one of the most influential stories in the world because of her impact on someone else's life. As you read the story, think about how you would have responded if you were in her situation:

- In 1866, she is born into an impoverished family.
- At age five she contracts trachoma, an eye disease that makes her nearly blind.
- Her mother dies when she is eight years old.
- Her father abandons her at age 10 and she is sent to the Tewksbury Almshouse (a house for the poor and destitute).
- She has had no schooling; she cannot read, write, or do math.
- At age 14, she wanted to escape her impoverished life. She heard about the Perkins School for the Blind in Boston, Massachusetts.
- She convinced a few influential people to help her enroll at the Perkins School.
- Because of her lack of social skills and any education, her first several years at the Perkins School were humiliating and challenging.
- At age 20, she graduated from the Perkins School for the Blind as valedictorian.

Let's pause here and think about what this girl accomplished. She was nearly blind. She was on her own from age 10 and financially destitute. She could not read, write, or do math. She had no social skills. She had no real support from anyone. The only thing she had going for her was her "belief" she could create a better life for herself. She had a power within that drove her to her goal. Ann Sullivan accomplished something that no one thought was possible. Ann Sullivan is a prime example of making the impossible, possible!

But now, the rest of the story:

- Shortly after graduation, Ann Sullivan was hired to teach a seven-year-old blind and deaf girl.

- This girl was spoiled, stubborn, and incorrigible. She had no desire to learn.

- The teaching strategies that were supposed to work were unsuccessful with this child.

- Sullivan made the decision to think outside the box. She got the girl to make associations between objects she was familiar with and common words. This worked very well. In just a few months, the little girl learned almost 600 words, some multiplication facts, and how to read Braille.

- Sullivan worked with the girl's parents to get her enrolled in the Perkins School.

- Sullivan accompanied the girl to Perkins and continued to teach her. This effort soon produced amazing results and both Sullivan and the girl became famous for the remarkable progress.

- Because of Ann Sullivan's tremendous effort, Helen Keller earned a degree from Radcliff College.

- Ann Sullivan and Helen Keller maintained a close, life-long companionship. Together they worked through many struggles and successes. Life was never really easy for either of them. Together, they continued to make the impossible, possible! They achieved beyond expectations.

Let's do a little analysis of this situation. Sullivan was nearly blind herself. At 20 years of age, she was hired to teach a seven-year-old who was incorrigible. None of the standard teaching methods for blind and deaf instruction worked. Keller did not want to learn. Often there were angry arguments between the two. Any outsider looking at the situation would say, "This task is impossible." But Ann Sullivan had the power within. She was determined to succeed. She had a belief in herself. She was going to do whatever it took to get Helen Keller to learn. Ann Sullivan had the power within. It turned out that Ann Sullivan was indeed a "miracle worker!"

Many of you reading this book feel as if you are experiencing very difficult or heartbreaking situations. I am not minimizing, in any way, your circumstances. No matter your circumstances, you can gain some strength from the story of Ann Sullivan and Helen Keller.

There are few circumstances worse than what Sullivan experienced growing up. She succeeded because of her belief in herself, her power within. Sullivan's self-efficacy pulled her out of a destitute condition. Sullivan's self-efficacy pulled Keller out of an appalling situation. If Ann Sullivan and Helen Keller can achieve beyond expectations in those circumstances, you can too!

People who achieve beyond expectations develop a trust and belief in their own abilities. Over time, they have learned they have the capacity to accomplish tasks because they have developed persistence and creative problem-solving skills. They have learned that there is *always* a way to successfully accomplish a task, they just must figure it out. They have the mindset: "I will persist until I find a way!"

~

"It is your passion that empowers you to be able to do that thing you were created to do."

T. D. Jakes

~

Your Challenge: Develop Your Power Within

You are in charge of you. Here are some questions that will help you discover the most powerful you! The answers to these questions will provide essential information so you can achieve beyond expectations by developing your power within. Write your responses in your journal.

1. Of the information you read in this chapter, what are the most important points to immediately apply to your life?

2. What specific strategies will you implement to strengthen your self-efficacy?

3. What action steps are you going to implement to be more confident as a person, as a parent, as a leader?

Remember, there is no quick fix when developing your self-efficacy. You are involved in a continuous, ongoing developmental process. You must be constantly self-assessing to determine the progress you are making. Take responsibility for and celebrate your progress. A high level of self-efficacy is the driving force to achieve beyond expectations.

∽

"Believe in your infinite potential.
Your only limitations are those you set upon yourself."

Roy T. Bennett

∽

Key Points: The Power Within

1. Self-efficacy is the belief you have in your ability to take on and successfully complete challenging tasks.
2. A high level of self-efficacy is what separates the extraordinary from the ordinary.
3. Bandura identified four sources of influence needed to develop self-efficacy:
   a. Mastery experiences—develop your expertise to become consciously competent about the knowledge, skill, and tactics necessary to accomplish your goal.
   b. Vicarious experiences provided by social models—create a vision for success by observing expert performances
   c. Social persuasion—expert constructive coaching to improve performance
   d. Interpreting emotional states—ability to understand and control your emotions
4. Enhance your self-efficacy by doing the following:
   a. Develop resilience
   b. Use creative higher-level thinking skills
   c. Use intrinsic motivation
   d. Develop an internal locus of control

~

"Ignite your power within to make
the impossible, possible!"
Bill Blokker, EdD

~

7

Train Your Brain

Make It Happen!

YOU HAVE the power within to control situations or control your reaction to situations. This book was written to inspire and inform you. What you choose to do with this information will determine your future. Your past is the past. Your future can be whatever you decide it to be.

In this book, you read about many people who conquered crushing obstacles. All of them achieved beyond expectations. They made the impossible, possible! You can too when you apply the specific, research-based information and strategies presented to help you master the five intangibles. In mastering these, you maximize your talent so you can achieve beyond expectations. Your future is in your hands.

For some of you, there may be some fear. You may think all of this information is overwhelming. You may be thinking, "There is so much to learn, where do I start?" If you are thinking those thoughts, that is normal. You're taking on a huge task. You're putting yourself out on the edge, beyond your comfort zone. But that is what all high achievers do! Remember, what matters in life it is not what happens, but *your reaction* to what happens.

Establish a positive mindset. You have the power within. You can take on this challenge and succeed. You can take one step at a time, just as the people highlighted in this book have done. To assist your quest for success, this chapter identifies the priority strategies to implement. By focusing on these, you will lay a solid foundation on which to apply all the other content and strategies in the coming months and years.

Here is a story that I believe will inspire your efforts. It is about a woman who had to train her brain so she could live a normal life.

In December 1996, she awoke with excruciating pain behind one of her eyes. A blood vessel had burst in her brain; she was very aware that she was having a stroke. She observed with amazement that her brain was shutting down. She was losing her ability to speak, read, write, and walk. She thought, "I am just an infant in a woman's body." Two and a half weeks after the stroke, doctors removed a blood clot from the left hemisphere of her brain the size of a golf ball.

Now what does she do? Remember her thinking, "I am just an infant in a woman's body"? That thought was very accurate, because after surgery nothing was working! She lost the ability to perform the absolute basics of living. Many people would intellectually and emotionally shut down. Quit!

Dr. Jill Bolte-Taylor made the decision that she was going to fully recover. She was going to train her brain. Taylor had dedicated her life to understanding problems with the brain and nervous system. Now she was going to learn about her brain from the inside out. She had to train her brain and nervous system in all the basic skills of life: speaking, reading, writing, walking. Just imagine the physical, intellectual, and emotional effort needed—learning to walk, learning to write, learning to read (text comprehension was her biggest challenge).

In addition, Dr. Taylor had to overcome the low expectations of her own doctors. Some of them told her that if she didn't relearn something within six months, she would never relearn it! It was overwhelming to say the least. To overcome all these immense challenges, Dr. Taylor needed a passion to succeed. She also needed the care and support of many people to accomplish these tasks. On many occasions, she was on the verge of giving up. This brain training process took Dr. Taylor eight years to completely recover all of her physical functions and thinking ability. There is no doubt Dr. Jill Bolte-Taylor achieved beyond expectations. She made the impossible, possible!

In her book, *My Stroke of Insight*, Dr. Taylor explains her recovery process. She provides a superb and detailed description of how she, along with those assisting her, trained her brain and nervous system. She knew it would be a long and arduous process, but the result would be worth all the effort.

Dr. Taylor's self-awareness skills were critical to her success. She was always monitoring herself and adjusting her thinking to ensure she would succeed. She and her team continually used emotional control skills. She had unbelievable self-efficacy. She was determined to return to her former self. Dr. Taylor overcame the low expectations of medical experts. She used incremental steps to accomplish huge goals. When she experienced the smallest successes, she would celebrate them.

Dr. Taylor's story provides a framework for this chapter. She had to train her brain. She had to relearn basic skills that normally are developed in the first few years of life. Taylor's story informs us of what is possible. It provides hope. It is possible to totally retrain your brain to accomplish your goals. If Dr. Taylor can do it in such extreme circumstances, so can you!

~

"Life isn't about finding yourself . . .
It's about CREATING yourself."
George Bernard Shaw

~

All the people highlighted in this book had to train their brains to accomplish their amazing feats. In the brain research, they talk about brain "plasticity." It means the brain has tremendous capacity to modify itself and how it works. This was evident in the case of Dr. Taylor. Even more dramatic results of brain plasticity have been reported in children who had half their brain surgically removed to stop epileptic seizures. Many of these children lead full and thriving lives no different from children who have not had the operation. The reason is our brain's plasticity, its ability to modify the way it functions.

Develop the Framework to Train Your Brain

You will be most effective training your brain for high achievement when you establish a framework to support your effort. The components of that framework have been derived from over 60 years of brain research.

We know the brain's number one priority is to ensure our physical survival. It reacts powerfully to every threat, whether it is physical or emotional. When it reacts this way, it triggers the entire body to prepare to fight or flee. When the brain and body are in this fight/flight mode, the brain focuses on nothing but survival. It ignores all other stimuli.

Next, the brain is a pattern maker. It is designed to cause us to operate efficiently. Once it recognizes what is important to us, it develops neural pathways that allow us to operate automatically and efficiently at a subconscious level.

Finally, in the absence of threat, the brain becomes goal oriented. It sorts stimuli to cause you to focus on whatever you have determined to be important in that immediate period of time. It knows what you want as a result of your repeatedly communicating to your brain an intention or desire and attaching positive emotion to it.

Understanding how the brain functions is important if you want the brain to learn anything new. We must create a framework for the brain to learn most effectively. The components of this framework to train your brain are:

1. Positive and Focused

2. Appropriate Challenge

3. Practice/Reinforcement to Mastery

4. Affirmations from Self and Others

1. Positive and Focused

    First, we need to create a safe environment, with an absence of threat. A positive, supportive atmosphere allows the brain to focus on what is to be learned. Learning is a risky business. When we learn, we step out and attempt to do something we have not done before. We therefore need to minimize any fear of failure by taking a step-by-step approach that maximizes the opportunity to succeed.

    Second, the brain needs a goal, task, or objective on which to focus. This goal setting process must include specifics about what you want to happen. Most importantly, you must attach strong, positive emotions to the goal. Focus on all the positive benefits of accomplishing the goal.

2. Appropriate Challenge

    Lev Vygotsky identified the Zone of Proximal Development (ZPD) in relation to teaching children. It can be applied in any learning situation with adults as well. The Zone of Proximal Development is defined as those behaviors a person can perform with a little assistance from an expert.

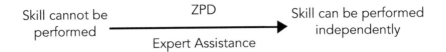

Skill cannot be performed → ZPD / Expert Assistance → Skill can be performed independently

    Consider this example. Let's say that, during a lecture, a medical student receives instructions on how to stitch a minor wound. Using a lifelike mannequin, she attempts to stitch a wound but is unsuccessful. The instructor observes the student's attempts and directs her to modify a hand movement as she does a stitch. As a result, with the instructor's assistance, the medical student performs the next set of stitches successfully. The ZPD was identified when the student could not perform the stitching. The instructor provided minor assistance and the student succeeded.

When learning a new skill, success is important. If people do not experience success during the learning process, they will not continue their attempts to learn. Vygotsky's research has been replicated and applied extensively in all walks of life. The coach/mentor finds out what the person can do, then uses a step-by-step approach to guide the person through the learning curve until they have mastered the new skill.

3. Practice/Reinforcement to Mastery

The purpose of practice and reinforcement is to develop mastery of the skill and become consciously competent. The new skill must be practiced over and over again to develop the habits to do it automatically, at a subconscious level. To develop true mastery of a skill, it must be practiced in real-life and increasingly difficult situations. This pragmatic approach provides a broad range of experiences that help you achieve mastery. In this process, you learn from both missteps and successes. It is essential you continually analyze your performance to determine what strategies are effective versus ineffective. This process causes you to become consciously competent, so you can repeat the behavior at will.

Mental rehearsal, also called visualization, is a great reinforcing strategy to apply when working to develop mastery of a skill. Aymeric Guillot, PhD, says visualization triggers the nervous system so your mental performance develops neural pathways just as you do when performing the actual activity. The basics of visualization are described in chapter 5, page 177.

Positive self-talk also plays an important role in reinforcing learning cues and success. There are three categories of self-talk you can use: cues/instruction for a specific activity, positive emotional support, and intrinsic rewards. Each of these is described on page 140.

4. Affirmations from Self and Others

Affirming and getting recognition for a job well done is essential to the learning process. We all need positive recognition for our efforts. During the learning process, it is important to experience both extrinsic and intrinsic rewards.

Extrinsic rewards come from the coach/expert communicating you have performed successfully. This extrinsic reward, recognition, must identify a specific skill or process you did well.

Intrinsic rewards come from within yourself. They are affirmations you provide to yourself. You express your pride in your success. You identify specific strategies or processes that you have performed successfully. Recognition and affirmations are essential to develop your skill to the mastery level.

Your success with training your brain is dependent on creating a framework with the characteristics just described. As evidenced in all the people whose stories were highlighted in this book, any change you want to make in your life is always going to involve brain training and assistance from both experts and emotional support people.

~

"What separates great players from the good ones is not so much ability as brain power and emotional equilibrium."

Arnold Palmer

~

The remainder of this chapter will synthesize and reinforce the foundational concepts you have read in each chapter and establish the priorities you need to pursue to train your brain to make them happen.

Chapter 1–Execution Transcends Talent

The two foundational concepts of this chapter are:

- No matter how much talent you have, your performance is determined by the five intangibles.

- The past is the past. You can't change it. Your future is a blank slate waiting for you to write the script.

What Separates the Extraordinary from the Ordinary?

No matter your role or responsibilities in life, we know we need to develop the technical knowledge and skill to perform. This essential training is the specialty of technical/vocational institutes, colleges, and universities. However, if you want extraordinary performance, you must train your brain to command the five intangibles. Execution transcends talent. Your execution is driven by your self-awareness, emotional control, habits, expectations, and self-efficacy. These intangibles power your performance and maximize your talent. Extraordinary people know that execution transcends talent.

~

Every dream has a process and a price tag.
Those who embrace the process and pay the price,
live the dream. Those who don't, just dream."
Jeremy Riddle

~

Your Past is Your Past, Your Future is Written by You

Here is a story of a man who trained his brain to make it happen! He ignored his past and wrote the script for his future. He literally made a 180-degree turn in his life.

Imagine that this is your life:

- You graduate from high school in a small town in Nebraska.
- Drugs and alcohol take over your entire life.
- A friend suggests robbing small-town banks for easy drug money.
- Do you do it?

Shon Hopwood did. In 1997 and 1998, Hopwood and a friend staged five small-town bank robberies across the state of Nebraska, stealing over $200,000. But their success was short lived. Hopwood was convicted and entered prison in May of 1999. He spent ten years in federal prison.

For many people, entering federal prison for a serious felony is the end of their story. But Hopwood wasn't like most prisoners. Instead of languishing over his poor decisions, he found something he loved.

Hopwood discovered a true passion for law. In the prison library, he read nonstop from books about the legal world and soon found himself as what's known as a "jailhouse lawyer"–an inmate whom other inmates come to for advice and guidance in their own cases. He was very, very good at it.

One fellow inmate had a request. He wanted the Supreme Court of the United States to hear his case, which requires a petition for certiorari. This is a formal, complex request for the Supreme Court to hear the case. Hopwood, with no legal education or experience, using a prison typewriter, wrote the petition. The Supreme Court received 7,209 petitions for certiorari in 2002. They heard eight cases. One was written by Shon Hopwood! The inmate in question had four years taken off his sentence.

A former US solicitor general soon took Hopwood under his wing, guiding and advising him. Hopwood took college classes in prison. "I kind of flourished there," he told the New York Times. "I didn't want prison to be my destiny. When your life gets tipped over and spilled out, you have to make some changes."

That's resilience. Shon learned that he had to monitor and adjust. This is a man who was an alcoholic and a drug addict. He robbed banks with a gun. Shon decided he was going to control the situation. He made the decision that he was always going to be the most prepared person in the room. When he emerged from prison, a paralegal job came next. Then law school.

It would have been understandable, maybe even expected, for a man like Shon Hopwood to slide back into his former life. But Shon's passion and persistence eventually allowed him to argue multiple cases in front of the Supreme Court.

Now, Hopwood is an associate professor of law at Georgetown University in Washington, D.C., one of America's most prestigious law schools. He's currently on track to become a tenured professor, teaching future lawyers about criminal justice reform and prisoners' rights. By training his brain, Shon Hopwood made the impossible, possible!

Think about all the ways Shon had to train his brain. He literally had to make a 180-degree turn in his life, away from being a criminal and toward becoming a lawyer. He had to master the five intangibles as he was developing his knowledge/skills related to the law and how to perform as an attorney. He had to train his brain to became more self-aware and to avoid emotion commotion. Hopwood had to create new habit patterns. He had to make sure that his high expectations controlled his reality.

~

"Though no one can go back and make a
brand-new start, anyone can start from now
and make a brand-new ending."

Carl Bard

~

Shon Hopwood, and all the other high achievers in this book, understand that the past is the past. It cannot be changed. The same is true for you! *No matter what has happened to you in the past, you can make your future much brighter.*

You can create your future. If you continue to do what you have done, you will get more of what you've got! Is that what you want? You are in charge. Your future is a blank slate waiting for you to write the script. Train your brain to focus on what you want. Train your brain to be passionate and positive about your future. Train your brain to find a way to succeed, no matter the obstacles that arise.

Chapter 2—Self-Awareness: Eliminate Your Blind Spots

Self-awareness is the single most important of the five intangibles because it alerts you to your emotions, thoughts, and behavior. Your number one priority is to train your brain to elevate your self-awareness related to the intangibles. Poor self-awareness means you have no control of the intangibles. The two foundational concepts for this chapter are:

- Self-awareness provides information to control the other four intangibles: emotions, habits, expectations, and self-efficacy.

- Self-awareness triggers the reticular activating system (RAS) and frontal lobe into action so you can control situations or your reaction to situations.

~

"As my awareness increases, my control
over my own being increases."
William Schutz

~

To establish the two foundational concepts, focus on these priorities:

- Continually monitor your self-talk.
- Continually monitor your emotions.

Monitor Your Self-Talk

Your self-talk is integral to your self-awareness. You are continually talking to yourself, no matter the situation, positive or negative. Your self-talk provides insights to your intellectual and emotional state. Your self-talk has two general functions:

1. Your self-talk reports your reactions to stimulus. You read about the Response to Perceived Threat on page 80. When you perceive a threat, you have an instinctive physical, emotional, and verbal reaction. Your verbal reaction, at this time, must be the trigger that stimulates your frontal lobe to activate.

2. Your self-talk can control your emotions and behavior. If you have positive self-talk, your brain and body provide you with the stimulus and information to be successful. If you have negative self-talk, your brain and body provide you with the stimulus and information to fail!

Whether you consciously pay attention to your self-talk or you don't, it still impacts your behavior. Your self-talk is a form of mind control! When you hear the same message again and again, you believe it, whether it is helpful or harmful. You must monitor and adjust your self-talk to ensure it is helping you achieve beyond expectations.

Is your self-talk controlling and reinforcing the behavior you want? If the answer is yes, continue to do what you are doing. If the answer is no, you must train your brain in new self-talk habit patterns. By establishing the new self-talk habit patterns, you will control and reinforce the behavior needed to succeed. To develop your new self-talk habits, use the Nine-Step Process to Replace a Habit in chapter 4, page 132.

Monitor Your Emotions

Your self-talk alerts you to your emotional state. When you first become aware of a challenging situation, you experience an emotion that is often transmitted to your consciousness by the expression of some type of self-talk. This is your early warning signal. It should immediately alert your RAS and frontal lobe that they need to step in and take charge. What matters in life is not what happens, but *your reaction* to what happens. An initial negative reaction is normal, but your RAS must use it to trigger your frontal lobe to take charge and regulate your emotional response.

Analyze your self-talk to determine if you need to train your brain.

- Is your self-talk positive?
- Does your self-talk help you stay calm in challenging situations?
- Does your self-talk reinforce your expectations of success?

You must train your brain for any question where you answered "no."

~

"Self-talk is the most powerful form of communication because it either empowers you or defeats you.'"
Wright Thurston

~

Your top two priorities are to focus your self-awareness on your self-talk and emotional reaction. After you have developed your new self-awareness habit patterns in those areas, you may want to focus on:

1. Eisenhower Priority Process (p. 57)
2. Values Conflicts (p. 51)

Increasing your self-awareness in these two areas will significantly assist your efforts to achieve beyond expectations. Both are important and at some time you must focus your self-awareness process on each of them.

Chapter 3–Avoid Emotion Commotion

Emotions are the most powerful of the five intangibles. Powerful emotions, positive or negative, paralyze performance. Your success in any endeavor is determined by your ability to regulate your emotions. Nothing positive occurs when your emotions are running rampant. Negative emotions create a toxic environment and incite further negativity. You must train your brain to regulate your emotions. By doing this, you will maximize the capacity of the most powerful intangible.

The most important foundational concept in chapter 3 is that *you are solely responsible for your emotions and the actions that result from them.*

You choose to act on an emotion. You are responsible for all you say or do. You cannot blame someone else for your behavior when it is triggered by your emotions. It is essential to become self-aware regarding your emotions and how you let them impact your behavior.

> *"No matter the situation, never let your emotions overpower your intelligence."*
>
> *KushandWizdom*

Your top priority is to avoid emotion commotion. To do that, you use the Five-Step Emotion Control Process. This process trains your brain to focus on a series of mental steps that cause you to use your frontal lobe to think logically to resolve challenging situations. Let's take another look at the Response to Perceived Threat graphic that you read about in chapter 3.

RESPONSE TO PERCEIVED THREAT

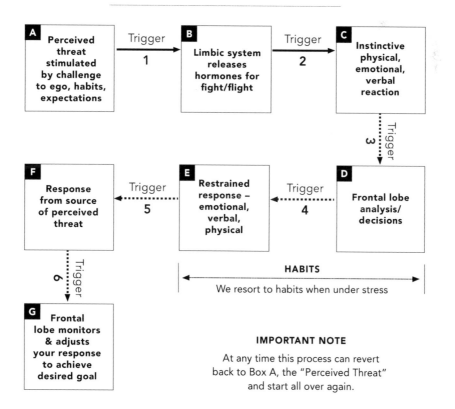

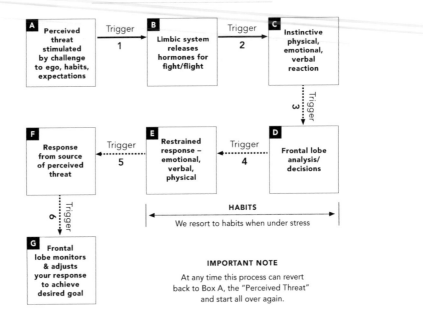

As you recall, Box C is your first opportunity to recognize your body is reacting to a stimulus. Self-awareness at this point is essential. If you recognize the first indicators of potential emotion commotion, you can take control before it takes control of you. To develop emotional control, you must recognize what triggers behavior so you know when to activate your frontal lobe. When the frontal lobe takes charge, you can decide how you are going to control the situation or how you are going to control your reaction to the situation.

Five-Step Emotion Control Process

1. *Awareness of the Trigger:* This is Box C in the Response to Perceived Threat—your instinctive physical, emotional, verbal reaction. You experience the initial emotional discomfort—confusion, frustration, worry, disbelief. *This is*

*the time you MUST activate your frontal lobe to take
control.*

2. *Pause*: This is Box D—frontal lobe stops all verbal reactions and body language. Here is where you may have to fight to push down your initial habitual response.

   a. *Use Self-Talk*: force and encourage your frontal lobe into action. Use positive and purposeful words to drive your behavior.

   b. *Remove* Your Ego: demand your frontal lobe control your limbic system and ego. Stop the fight/flight thinking. Use logic to determine what is best to improve this situation for both short and long term.

   c. *Think*: give the frontal lobe time to think. What is the best result I can get in this situation? What behavior is going to get me the results I want?

   d. *Decide*: force your frontal lobe into action. You have monitored and now you are going to adjust your behavior to get the best results for this situation.

3. *Act*: This is Box E—be confident, positive and purposeful. You are now acting out of logic rather than emotion. You can succeed.

4. *Monitor*: This is Box F—your frontal lobe activates your external self-awareness to determine how your words and actions impact the others.

5. *Adjust*: This is Box G—your frontal lobe uses self-awareness data to determine what you need to do/say to keep moving forward on a positive course.

The Five-Step Emotion Control Process prompts self-awareness of your habits in stressful situations. The five-step process can be applied in less than 10 seconds. It guides your use of the frontal lobe. It gives you the opportunity to develop new habit patterns if you so choose. Use these self-talk key words to prompt your behavior:

1. Trigger
2. Pause—Think
3. Act
4. Monitor
5. Adjust

Once you have trained your brain to use the Five-Step Emotion Control Process, you must decide what other information from chapter 3 you want apply to your life. There are three specific sections that people tell us are the most useful:

- Controlling Common Negative Emotions—Fear (p. 94)
- Controlling Common Negative Emotions—Anger (p. 97)
- Stress in Your Life—Eustress or Distress (p. 105)

~

"If you fail to control how you think, you will fail!"
Bill Blokker, EdD

~

Chapter 4—Habits: Your Hidden Mind Chains

Habits are hidden mind chains that control 40%-75% of your daily behaviors. You resort to habits any time you are under pressure. You must decide, are your habits helping or hindering you in stressful situations?

Habits and negative emotions working together create immense problems. Your priority is to determine if your emotional habits are creating self-imposed barriers. On page 142, the Emotional Habit Activity will open your eyes to those hidden mind chains that paralyze your behavior. You will find out if your emotional habits are creating problems for you.

Your second priority is to train your brain in the Nine-Step Process to Replace a Habit on page 132.

~

"I have learned that champions aren't just born; champions can be made when they embrace and commit to life-changing positive habits."

Lewis Howes

~

Once you have implemented the first two priorities above, you can focus on the Foundational Habits to Make the Impossible, Possible, on page 144:

1. Passion as a habit

2. Positivity as a habit

3. Time Management as a habit

4. Resilience as a habit

5. Action Orientation as a habit

6. Intuition as a habit

7. Persistence as a habit

Chapter 5–Expectations Determine Your Reality

Expectations determine your reality. You just need to decide which expectations you will allow to determine your reality. Holding high expectations for yourself is the only way you can achieve your full potential. Having high expectations may frighten you. That's okay. Nothing of value is achieved in this world without causing you to stretch and feel discomfort.

The two foundational concepts in this chapter are:

- Become aware of and reject any expectations from society or significant others that do not support the high expectations you have of yourself.

- Focus on those thoughts and behaviors needed to accomplish your high expectations.

Your top priority is to train your brain in the five strategies used by high achievers to accomplish their huge goals (page 172).

Strategy 1: Dream Big
Strategy 2: Use Incremental Goal Setting
Strategy 3: Use Your Frontal Lobe to Avoid
    Emotion Commotion
Strategy 4: Use Positive Self-Talk
Strategy 5: Visualize the Dream

~

"Risk more than others think is safe.
Care more than others think is wise.
Dream more than others think is practical.
Expect more than others think is possible."

Claude Bissell

~

After you have become consciously competent with these five strategies, you can look at ways to minimize the implementation dip when making a change. Train your brain to understand Tuckman's four developmental stages everyone goes through to accomplish a high expectation. Train your brain in the strategies to minimize the impact of the implementation dip in the Forming, Storming, and Norming stages

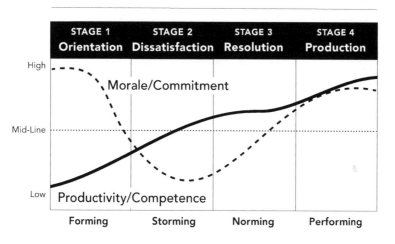

TUCKMAN'S DEVELOPMENTAL STAGES OF A GROUP

When you expect and are prepared for this implementation dip, you will reduce many of the self-imposed barriers that can paralyze your performance.

Chapter 6–Self-Efficacy: The Power Within

Self-efficacy is the belief you have in your ability to take on and successfully complete challenging tasks. Self-efficacy is what drives you to make the impossible, possible.

The foundational component of this chapter is that *self-efficacy results when you train your brain to become consciously competent about the knowledge, skills, and tactics necessary to accomplish your goal.* The more consciously competent you become, the greater your self-efficacy.

The two most important priorities to develop self-efficacy are:

- Resilience
- Using creative, higher-level thinking skills

Resilience

Resilience is your ability to rebound from any malfunction with optimism and energy. Your resilience is dependent on your:

- Self-awareness
- Goal commitment
- Emotional control
- Action orientation
- Creative problem solving
- Tenacity

In chapter 6, there is a chart on page 219 that identifies each of these characteristics and lists behaviors for each. Use this chart as your "recipe" for resilience. You can follow the recipe any time you are in a difficult situation. It will both inform and inspire you to perform at your highest level.

Creative, Higher-Level Thinking Skills

The process of setting high expectations for yourself ensures you will encounter many perplexing problems that must be resolved. Expect this. Prepare for this. To resolve these problems, you must develop your higher-level thinking skills of analysis, evaluation, and synthesis as described in Bloom's Taxonomy—Levels of Thinking on page 222.

This Levels of Thinking chart provides you direction for how to work through challenging situations. Remember, the most important thing you must do is *keep a positive mindset*. Your brain can perform at a high level *only* when you have a positive state of mind.

~

"Your thoughts can shape your feelings, can shape your actions. Thinking is powerful stuff whether you're shaping your moment, or shaping your lifetime."

J. D. Meier

~

You Can Achieve Beyond Expectations

You can make the impossible, possible. You have the power within when you train your brain to be your ally rather than your opponent. Your self-awareness is the most important intangible needed to succeed. You must train your brain to continually monitor and adjust all aspects of your behavior to ensure you're getting the results you want.

Whenever you work to make the impossible, possible, you will experience negative reactions. It is inevitable. You are putting yourself on the edge. It's going to be difficult, scary, stressful, and frustrating. Making the impossible, possible is going to put a strain on all of your senses.

Emotion is the most powerful intangible. Emotion can either paralyze you or fan the flames for success. You can control your emotions. You must control your emotions. You must develop and continually refine your emotional control skills. By doing so, you will have the tools to ensure you can control situations or your reactions to situations.

In this book, you read about many people achieving beyond expectations. They are inspirational examples of how to make the impossible, possible. Whenever you start to feel the emotion commotion setting in, remind yourself of what you read about the people in this book. Compare your situation to theirs. If they could succeed in their catastrophic conditions, you can succeed in yours. You have the power within. You can achieve beyond expectations.

~

You Were Meant for Greatness

You are stronger, smarter and more
resilient than you think.
You are capable of achieving far more than you believe.
You were meant for greatness—like all of those who
have achieved it. But, it takes persistence.
It takes determination.
It takes facing your fears and doing that which is hard
and necessary, instead of what is quick and easy.
It takes skipping the mythical shortcuts and
using your imagination as a map and
preview of life's coming attractions.

Zero Dean

~

Acknowledgments

MANY PEOPLE contributed to the development of this book. They fall into two categories: 1) people who contributed in some way to the content of the book; and 2) people who had a hand in the refinement of and publishing of the book.

Most of the people in the first group have no idea that they were contributing. I want to recognize and thank each of them. Some of these people mentored and challenged me to be the best I could be. Others I was able to observe and learn from as they struggled to overcome life's challenges.

First, I want to recognize the people identified or highlighted in this book. Their amazing accomplishments in the face of such crushing obstacles provides the inspiration for each of us. They showed us that you can achieve beyond expectations, no matter your circumstances. Their stories remove excuses any of us may have. They have demonstrated that you can make the impossible, possible!

I must acknowledge and thank my wife, Sue. She has been at my side during college and my entire professional career. She has supported and encouraged me in every endeavor, no matter how risky. During that time, we struggled together to overcome challenges related to raising children, relationships, finances, family, and running our businesses. Together we founded and grew two very successful businesses. She modeled the five intangibles on-a-daily basis. Sue was her very best when we had significant obstacles to overcome. Sue has contributed to this book in so many ways. I am indebted to her. Together, we have achieved beyond expectations.

Sue and I have two sons Kevin and Scott. At an early age, they began applying the five intangibles. They excelled both academically and athletically in high school and college. Now, both are in significant leadership positions in large businesses. Observing them set high expectations and then work through all the challenges to succeed has both informed and inspired me. Both Kevin and Scott demonstrated over-and-over again that execution transcends talent. Both should be very proud of all they have accomplished. I know their Mom and I are.

Dick Lyons was my college football coach. Donald Distin and Burton Ramer, Ed.D. were two of my bosses. All three, mentored me and modeled for me the application of the five intangibles. They taught me how to set high expectations and then monitor and adjust my behavior until I succeeded.

John Morford, EdD, and Roy Wahle, PhD, made significant contributions to this book and my professional career. Morford created the Educational Leadership program at Seattle University. Wahle was my major advisor. Both men molded, shaped, and crystalized my understanding of leadership and human performance. During my three years earning my doctorate, they guided me through intense, real-life application of all the concepts identified in this book. It was the most significant learning experience in my life. Because of their efforts, I have been able to positively impact the lives of thousands of people. I will be forever grateful to Dr. Morford and Dr. Wahle for their significant contributions to my personal and professional life.

When I began writing this book there were two people who played significant roles: Cassandra Woody and Sam Osterling. Cassandra was the first one to provide me with editorial direction to begin this effort. She was most patient and understanding and got me moving in the right direction. She was the catalyst for me to continue my efforts. Sam provided substantial help pulling together information about the people highlighted in this book. His enthusiasm and dedication created the groundwork for the inspirational stories in this book.

Last, but not least, are Sandra Beckwith, Sharon Scroggins, and Debbie Whitfill. At various times during this process, each of them read and provided their candid observations about both the content and writing style. In each case, I paid careful attention to what they were telling me. All three were very generous with their time to provide meaningful feedback.

Now I must acknowledge all those who have contributed to the publication of this book. Rick Benzel, publisher of New Insights Press, did the heaviest lifting. He had the tough job of molding, shaping, and editing my original writing and re-writes into the final product that would effectively inspire and inform the reader. Rick and I had many in-depth discussions about both content and style. I think we both can be proud of the result of our efforts.

Brett Hullinger put the finishing touches on the book with his copyediting skills.

Finally, Susan Shankin created a marvelous cover and interior design that transformed the manuscript into a beautiful and readable book.

As you have read in this book, all great achievements are a team effort. The people I have acknowledged were significant team members who contributed to this book. I am thankful I have had the opportunity to work with each of them.

About the Author

BILL BLOKKER, EdD, is an example of achieving beyond expectations. He practices what he preaches. Blokker studied high achieving people and organizations when earning his doctorate in leadership and organizational development from Seattle University. For over 30 years, he has applied the five intangibles when directing individual and organizational transformation. In business, he founded two successful companies. One he grew into the top 2% performing companies in the United States.

Blokker has drawn on all his personal, educational and professional experience when writing this book. Bill knows firsthand what separates the extraordinary from the ordinary. The book is a no-nonsense wake-up call designed to inspire and inform. He describes how the high achievers highlighted in this book conquered crushing obstacles by igniting their power within. Blokker provides practical strategies to trigger extraordinary performance. Bill inspires you to make the impossible, possible.

For more information, go to:
www.achievebeyondexpectations.com

For questions, comments or inquires contact Bill at:
bill@achievebeyondexpectations.com

Made in the USA
Coppell, TX
21 September 2020

38506744R00166